DEVELOPMENT AND INTEGRATION OF NEPALI CULTURE IN ASSAM

About the Author

K.K. Muktan, a retired bureaucrat turned author, was born and brought up in Assam, North East India in 1931. After graduating from St. Anthony's College, Shillong in 1953 he did his M.A. in Economics from the Allahabad University and joined Assam Civil Service (ACS) in 1960. On bifurcation of Meghalaya from Assam Mr. Muktan was absorbed in the Meghalaya Civil Service (MCS) in 1975. He retired from service in 1989.

Having been closely associated with the activities of socio-economic development of people throughout his service life, Mr. Muktan is deeply interested in the dynamics of Indian society in general and Nepali community in particular. He has conducted research work on Tamang society and written books. As the Adviser of the Meghalaya Pensioners' Association he has been serving the cause of retired pensioners and the aged. Mr. Muktan has to his credit a number of books such as – *The Legendary Gorkhas, Planning for Retirement, The Gorkhas in the Freedom Struggle of India, Indo Nepalese Socio-cultural Dimension, Origin and History of Tamang People* and many articles in News papers and Magazines.

DEVELOPMENT AND INTEGRATION OF NEPALI CULTURE IN ASSAM

K.K. Muktan

CONCEPT PUBLISHING COMPANY PVT. LTD.
NEW DELHI - 110 059

ISBN: 978-93-6344-757-8

First Published 2025

Published and Printed by

Since 1974

Concept Publishing Company Pvt. Ltd.
A/15-16, Commercial Block, Mohan Garden
New Delhi-110059 (India)
T: +91-11-41101460
E: publishing@conceptpub.com, *W*: www.conceptpub.com

Cataloging in Publication--Courtesy: D.K. Agencies (P) Ltd. <docinfo@dkagencies.com>

Muktan, K. K., author.
Development and integration of Nepali culture in Assam / K.K. Muktan.
pages cm
Includes bibliographical references and index.
ISBN 9789363447578

1. Nepali people--India--Assam--History. 2. Gorkha (South Asian people)--India--Assam--History. 3. Nepali people--India--Assam--Economic conditions. 4. Nepali people--Government policy--India--Assam. 5. Nepali people--India--Assam--Social life and customs. 6. Assam (India)--Social life and customs. I. Title.

LCC DS432.N46M85 2025 | DDC 305.891495054162 23

Foreword

"Great works are performed not by strength but by perseverance", Samuel Johnson... aptly mirrors the persona of Late K.K. Muktan—a retired bureaucrat, author, social worker, a philanthropist and a prolific writer, held in high esteem particularly in Meghalaya and Assam. I personally knew him for more than three decades and always admired him for his dedicated and selfless service to society. Though not directly into classroom academics, his writings have made an immense impact on people's lives. The present book has been written with in-depth insight and candor on the subject, thoroughly researched and involves a deep sense of interest and commitment to changing the world view of the Gorkha community with reference to the present scenario where its contributions have not been able to find a deserving space in the annals of Indian history.

The author talks about the presence of the Gorkhas in Assam, their origin and how they learnt to adapt and assimilate into the Assamese society. They immigrated not to rule but to look for livelihood opportunities. They survived and thrived through centuries from the time the Gorkhas of Cuttack Legion (later changed to Sylhet Light Infantry) first landed in Assam during 1817, the period marked by Burmese invasion. They played a pivotal role in providing protection to the

Assamese community from Burmese oppression. The Nepalese community was also actively involved in the Indian Freedom struggle and contributed towards the society which they regarded as their own. They integrated with the indigenous social and cultural fabric embracing and absorbing the beauty of the local traditions, beliefs and rituals while preserving their own culture, tradition and language.

The author paints a lucid picture of the assimilation of immigrants from various parts of North-east India and the Nepalese community in particular into the emerging Asamiya society. He has written a book that everyone can read and easily understand the complex yet undeniably simple interchange of cultures between communities over centuries. Wherever the Gorkhas are found to have settled, they are known to have adjusted with the lifestyle and culture of the local community yet they still face an identity crisis as the language they speak has always been an assumption in inferring their nationality.

The author's writings, meticulously documented, offer tools for further discussions on the subject which have opened avenues for research on the Gorkha community. He provides a vast information for those who are interested in the evolution of the Nepalese in the Northeastern region of the country. The book ends on an optimistic note with the possibility of the Gorkha community in India being studied and documented for posterity, with the belief that their existence and contributions will be acknowledged and genuinely appreciated.

The author undoubtedly is a pride of the region and the Gorkha community, deeply respected for his incredible work. I am deeply touched by his desire to constantly strive to make a better tomorrow. The book "Development and Integration of Nepali Culture in Assam" is a " Must Read" as the book is written with clarity and conviction on the emergence of the Gorkha community as an integral part of Northeast India.

Late K.K. Muktan—you will continue to be a source of inspiration for generations to come.

Shillong, March 2025

Prof. S.R. Joshi, FNASc
North-Eastern Hill University
Shillong, Meghalaya

Preface

Writing a preface for a book not authored by me is the most unexpected favour I have ever received in my life! So quite naturally, I take this as a golden chance to express my sweet memories of a man who at the ripe age of 94 years, has penned down each line and passage of this monograph with the calmness of his nature, the wisdom of his intellect and the silent voice of contemplation.

Writing was Daddy's passion and writing specifically on the Gorkhas was a subject most dear to him. In his own words he once said

> "Let me tell my readers that to me the life and history of the Nepalis/Gorkhas who have contributed their might with their labour, sweat, and blood have always been of deepest interest to me—I admit that this work of mine is but a spade work far from being exhaustive and I hope it generates interest among young scholars for further research in the foreseeable future."

The book is replete with historical evidences of assimilation of the Nepali migrants into Assamese culture. The merger or absorption was to the extent of sharing common religious faith, observance of festivals and ideals of universal brotherhood (*vasudhaiva kutumbakam*). The book deals with the deep annals of history of the Gorkha recruitment in the Indian army which started from 1815, a year before the signing of the ignominious treaty of Segowlee between Nepal Durbar and East India Company. Coming down to the medieval period the Nepalese migration into Assam tracing back to the fifteenth century the book delves into the push factors that played a role in the process of migration such as increasing fragmentation of land, heavy exploitation of landless tenants, ecological crisis, poverty, etc. On the other hand, the pull factors from India that encouraged large scale migration relates to Colonial patronage and wider scope for economic opportunities. Withstanding all this came in the rise to power by a section of Nepalis who became politically conscious and took part in the first general elections in the country in 1952. Another notable feature of the book is the highlight on the publication of a number of Nepali literature through books, articles and poems in Assamese language which in turn contributed to the already existing wealth of Assamese literature.The book discusses at length the contribution of Nepalis to the passing of the Official Language Bill, 1960 and the Assam Movement.

Needless to say this book in a nutshell gives a bird's-eye view of the socio-economic and political scenario of Nepalis and Assamese culture which no doubt will surely be of interest to young scholars working on areas such on cultural integration and assimilation as well as development studies.

I end my preface with a fervent hope that the candle of wisdom from my father will carry on its spark to future generations. This may be the last book ever written by my late father but the song by Neil Young rings a note in my ear as I sing. "May your hands always be busy.... May you stay forever young."

Alpine Villa, Shillong **Rekha Muktan Shangpliang**

Acknowledgements

If there is one reason why this book will have a very special place amongst the collection of books stacked in our home library, it is because this is the last book written by my dearest father. It has been long in the making shortly after the release of his previous three volume book *The Comprehensive History of the Nepalis in North-East India*. Over the years through his long journey, Daddy has crossed a number of people whose acquaintances, friendship, knowledge and support has enriched his life in so many ways.

First and foremost we give all glory and honour to our Lord and Saviour Jesus Christ for His love and blessing showered upon our Daddy that he could live a full and fruitful life. During the course of his writing there were many occasions when his health failed, but his trust and faith in God helped him overcome the most difficult situations. Daddy's long cherished desire to contribute more to the literature on the Gorkhas in the North-East led him to bring out a series of publications one after another.

I would be failing in my duty if I did not mention the immediate response given by the publisher Mr. Ashok Mittal who assured my father about the timely publication at a time when my father spoke to him about this book. I could see the curiosity and anticipation in him when he sent the first draft of this book to the publisher and Lo and Behold! here is the book published as promised.

With a humble heart, I start by thanking everyone who have known Daddy and who have in some way been instrumental in his life. To all those who have in some way or another been a blessing and a source of moral support to my father, I take this opportunity to thank you, on behalf of my family members, with deepest gratitude. Our sincere thanks goes to Professor Santaram Joshi, a family friend for many years, a special academician friend of my father who so willingly agreed to write the foreword of this book in spite of his busy schedule.

Our paternal and maternal relatives have been a constant support to Daddy making frequent phone calls to enquire about his health, so thankful to them for always being there. Daddy's grandchildren have been his biggest source of joy—he spent long hours with Abigail, Ethan and Elaine telling them stories from *Mahabharata* and *Ramayana*—At times even letting out the child in him as he once tried cycling with the kids while on a picnic. His love and concern for Cheryl, Daryl, Rachel, Stephanie, Jonathan and their lovely kids who are abroad kept him busy on international calls every now and then. At Melanie's wedding he looked ever handsome in his grey suit, making sure he gifted little Charlotte a silver spoon on her first birthday and of course the list would be endless to describe the overall support from his children Hima, Lolita, Anjalee and myself and his in-laws Tutu, Judy, Albert and Shem who have been constantly with him through thick and thin.

Last but not the least, this book would not have seen the light of the day if not for God Almighty on whom we place all our glory and honour.

Prof. Rekha M. Shangpliang
(Youngest daughter)

Contents

1

Introduction

The history of human civilisation is, essentially, the story of immigration and assimilation of different peoples. Like the waters of small streams that flow into the rivers and make greater water body, so also human civilisation, cultures and traditions meet together, assimilate and make richer and bigger culture. The history is replete with the accounts of great many peoples who migrated and settled down in alien countries, and in course of time, got themselves assimilated with the people and culture of the country. Inversely, there were also people who settled down in foreign country and prevailed upon the indigenous people of that land, and thrust upon them their own culture, language and religion. It was immaterial whether they came as peaceful settlers or as invaders: whether they settled down subtly and peacefully or subjugated the people and ruled over the country, but it was their cultures that played determinant role. Let us take, for example, the case of our own country, India. Over the past millennia India has come in contact with a numerous alien peoples, cultures and traditions which have influenced the course of life of the Indian people and left an indelible mark in their culture and history. India had a long cultural intercourse with western Asia ever since the invasion by the Persian king Darius in 510 BC who annexed Indus valley and made it the twentieth province of the Persian empire. The Persians that ruled over the north-western India for a period of nearly two centuries made a profound impact upon the life and culture of Indian people. Their Kharoshti script, an off-shoot of Aramaic language, came to be in vogue as official language in the north-western frontiers for several centuries. The Indo-Persian trade that developed between the two countries had a tremendous impact on the art, architecture and the lifestyle of the people of both India and Iran. According to B.N. Luniya, the Persian style of architecture influenced the art of the Mauryan architecture as reflected in the lion capitals of the Ashokan pillars.[1]

Similarly, the Greek settlement in Indian frontiers around 300 BC accelerated Indo-Greek trade and commerce which left a direct and visible mark on India's art and culture. The emergence of the Graeco-Buddhist art of Gandhara in India is an example of culture fusion, the traces of which are still to be seen in various caves and temples of India. The Greek rulers, whom the Hindus called Yavanas, not only brought their culture to India but also succumbed themselves to the fascination of Indian culture and embraced the religion of India. Menander, for example, the Greek ruler in India became a devout Buddhist under the noted Buddhist monk named Nagasena who is referred to as Milinda in popular Buddhist legend and regarded as a saint by the Buddhists. Heliodorus, the Greek ambassador of King Antialcidas embraced Hinduism, as a staunch believer in Visnu. The Shakas or Scythians who came to India from Central Asia established their supremacy over Indian people and ruled northern India, were influenced by Indian culture and religion and became converted into Buddhism and Hinduism. The Kushanas, after having pushed the Shakas towards South India, established their sway over the entire North India and ruled for a long time but eventually became converted to Buddhism and entirely assimilated with Indians. The great king Kanishka of Kushana dynasty not only embraced Buddhism but also patronized Buddhism and held the fourth Buddhist Council in India. Then followed the Turkish, Afghans and the Mughals who reigned over India for several centuries. The Muslim religious bigotry and biased administration of some rulers notwithstanding, India's religion, culture and language remained in tact. There were, no doubt, a lot of damage and destructions of Hindu temples and shrines but these were revived again and India's religion and culture sustained.

Let us take a closer view of Assam, our own state. Early in the thirteenth century an offshoot of the great Tai or Shan race called Ahom crossed over Patkai hill on the eastern border of Assam and settled down in the eastern valley of Brahmaputra named Tipam. They called Assam '*Mungdunsunkham*' (country of gold). They had their own language, faith, culture and highly developed history which they called 'Buranji'. They were politically and socially well-organised people with king as the head of the state, Priest(*Dewdhai*), nobles and a hierarchical set of officers. The Ahoms subdued the local tribes like the Asamiyas, Mataks, Morans, Chutias, Kacharis and ruled over Assam for nearly six hundred years from 1228 to 1826 AD. But despite being a powerful race they succumbed to the language, religion and tradition of the local indigenous people of Assam. King Siva Singha, son of Rudra Singha took the fascination for Saktism, the Brahminic style of worship of Durga and became the first Ahom king to be converted himself to Hinduism. He made Hinduism the state religion and performed sacrifices with the help of 108 Brahmins in his proselytising ceremony held at Biswanath temple. From the fourteenth century onward Assam passed through a strong devotional wave when the two sects of Hinduism, i.e., Saktism and Vaisnavism flourished side by side. Brahmins belonging to either sects poured into Assam from various places of India like, Mithila, Kanyakubja, Bonga etc. and proselytised the people of Assam into Hinduism. Siva Singha brought Krishnaram Bhattacharjya, a Brahmin priest from Nawadeep (Bengal) and became his disciple. He caused his nobles and officers to follow the suit. The Koch kings and the Ahom kings encouraged incoming of these Brahmins. When mass Ahom people accepted Hinduism, their tribal priests (*Dewdhais*) and Bailungs fell into disrepute and although they tried their best to resist the proselytising efforts of the Brahmins, they had, at last, to give way and become themselves 'Gisains'. Their sordid fanaticism touched the nadir when Phuleswari Devi, a temple dancer turned queen, ordered the Moamorias and Gosains to be brought to a Sakta shrine where sacrifices were being offered, and caused the distinguishing mark of the Sakta sect to be smeared with the blood upon their foreheads. The Moamorias could not bear this outrageous insult and broke into country-wide rebellion. Hinduism and the Brahminic traditions came to be practised by the mass people and the Sanskritised Assamese language became the lingua-franca. Gradually, the rising generation started forgetting Ahom language, culture and tradition due to long disuse. During the advent of the British in 1826 only a few old *Dewdhais* knew Ahom language through whom the British historians tried to translate the valuable Ahom Buranjis. This is how the "unequalled"and glorious Tai Ahom race who ruled Assam for long six hundred years gradually forgot their own language, culture and religion and passed into "decay in the sleepy hollow of the Brahmaputra valley"[2] as they became degenerated and completely assimilated with Asamiya culture and religion.

The Nepalis came to Assam, nearly two hundred years ago, not to rule over Assam like the Ahoms but to find their livelihood. The Gorkhas of Cuttack Legion (later changed the name to Sylhet Light Infantry) set their feet on the soil of Assam for the first time in 1817 during the wake of Burmese invasion of Assam. The Gorkhas were instrumental in driving away the Burmese and saving the Assamese people from their barbaric oppression. The Gorkhas came to Assam as recruits in the Indian army and subsequently as civilian immigrants and settled down permanently in Assam. They are multi-cultural and multi-lingual like Assamese people. They have their religion similar (or almost similar) to the Assamese people, their language Nepali born out of the same root (Sanskrit) and their customs and traditions not very different from the people of Assam. Historically speaking, a large section of them, belonging to Tibeto-Burman linguistic group had their origin in Assam. They were the descendants of Kirata race and their king Ghataka ruled over Kamrupa with his capital at Pragjyotisa[3], who was slain by Naraka. Subsequently, the Kiratas were pushed towards Nepal, Bhutan and the sub-Himalayan regions by the Aryans as they marched into the North Eastern India. Thus, the Nepali's migration into the North East was like their home coming.

As per historical evidences, ever since medieval times the Nepalese have been migrating and settling down in Assam and assimilating with the Assamese people. Initially, the migration was very small in number, unlike the large scale immigration of the present day. The movement of people from Nepal took place for many reasons such as—pilgrimage to religious places, matrimonial alliances, roving saints and seers. Common border and proximity, shared history, language and culture were other factors for movement of Nepalese into Assam. Reliable historical records are available about matrimonial alliances between the royal families of Nepal and those of Kamrupa. The daughter of Harsha Deva, the king of medieval Kamrupa was married to Jayadeva II, king of Nepal.[4] Even earlier than this, King Harsa Vardhana of Kamrupa is said to have married a Nepali princess in 153 AD. Later in sixteenth century AD, Biswa Singh, the founder of Koch kingdom, married Ratnakanti, the daughter of Nepal's king Ratnamalla.[5] King Biswa Singh made offerings of two golden umbrellas one each at Pasupatinath Temple and Gujyeswari temple of Nepal. After the death of king Biswa Singh his son, begotten from queen Ratnakanti, Malladev Singh ascended the throne who became famous in the history of Koch dynasty as king Naranarayana. It is said that the Koch kings brought from Nepal to his kingdom, a number of Brahmin priests, wood work artisans, stone and metal sculptors and a host of other workers.[6] The frequent royal matrimonial alliances, as referred to above, undoubtedly promoted lasting peace and friendship between the royal families which augmented trade relations between the two countries resulting in free movement of people and settlement into one another's territory. It is most probable that many of these people who migrated from Nepal and settled down in Assam must have completely merged and assimilated with the Assamese people. Many of them might have merged with Asamiya, some other with Koch, Kacharis, Meches etc. It is said that the Morans of Upper Assam were originally the people of Nepal; they came to settle down in Assam and became Assamese beyond recognition. Similarly we learn from Dr. Tirthanath Sarma, former President of Asom Sahitya Sobha that some Nepalese came to Assam during or little before the period of Neo-Vaishnavite movement and settled down in Assam. Among them there was one Nepali Brahmin named Rati Kanta Upadhyaya who was deeply involved in the process of setting up and development of Vaishnavite Satras. He was a devout follower of Sankardev and he founded two Satras, one at Tiyak of Sibsagar district and another at Nowgaon and himself became a Satradhikar. These two Satras are known as Nepali Satras even to this day. This palpable evidence goes to prove the fact, beyond doubt, that the Nepalis had entered the sanctum sanctorum of Assamese society and established their root in the soil of Assam at the very rudimentary period of Assamese Vaishnavite tradition. Shrimanta Sankardev (1449–1568) an Assamese polymath, a saint scholar, poet, playwright and a socio-religious reformer, propagated Neo-Vaishnavite movement in Assam which is the living tradition of Assamese people of today. Rati Kanta Upadhyaya, the Satradhikar became completely assimilated and merged with Assamese society leaving no trace of Nepali identity. Dr.Tirthanath Sarma rightly presumed, that a host of the Assamese Gokhains of today including Professor Jyotindra Nath Goswami, the three time Secretary of the Asom Sahitya Sobha might, in all probability, be the descendants of this Nepali Satradhikar of the 16th century of which they were blissfully unaware.[7]

In this context, Kanaklal Baruah in his article—"My Reminiscence", in *The Studies in Early History of Assam,* Edt. by Maheswar Neog, 1973, has stated as follows:

> "Evidently, in those days the process of assimilating new immigrants into the indigenous society had been quite quick. This process has been going on in Assam since time immemorial and it is still working well in Assam. It is this process that the Assamese Hindu society has been built up, that explains the complete fusion of the Gadiya, Utkal, Dravidi, Kamrupi, Maithili, Kanajia, Marwari and Gorkha Brahmin in the Assamese Brahmin society of the present day."[8]

As mentioned above by Kanaklal Baruah, it is understood that during the initial growth of Hinduism in Assam many Brahmins from Mithila and Kanyakubja (Kanauj) came to settle in Assam. Dr. Hutton in his—*Study on the Races and Religion in India,* stated—"Brahmins and Kayasthas of Assam are all imported from Northern India, mostly from North Bihar (Mithila) but the Assamese Kolita Brahmins are indigenous to Assam."[9] The Koch and Ahom kings became great patrons of Hinduism and encouraged Brahmins to come from Mithila of whom some were Nepali Brahmins. In ancient times Mithila total (Tirhut or Trabhukti) was situated on the border between north Bihar and Nepal. Even today, as many as eight districts of Nepal, such as, Dhanusa, Mahottari, Rautahat, Saptari, Sarlahi etc. form part of Maithili speaking region. E.A.Gait stated—"a Kshatriya named Dharma Pal came from west and founded a kingdom, west of Guwahati and attracted thither a number of Brahmins and other high-caste Hindus from upper India. The sage Kendu Kulai is said to have lived in this reign. He was succeeded in turn by Padma Narayan, Chandra Narayan and others, ending with Ram Chandra whose capital was at Ratnapur in the Majuli."[10] According to Manirul Hussain—"those Nepalese who migrated from Nepal in limited number gradually assimilated with the emerging Asamiya society, abandoned their past Nepali identity[11] and became pure Assamese.

Thus, in the earlier days, the process of assimilation of Nepalis, as stated above, was total and complete. The merger or absorption into Asamiya culture was to the extent of complete extinction of their Nepali culture, tradition and language. This could happen in those days because, the number of migrants was small and the ethnic consciousness among them was not much strong. They were carried away by religious fetish and the ethos of universal brotherhood (*Vasudhaiva kutumbakam*) that was at the uppermost in those days. History gives us evidences of many tribes or communities that assimilated with other larger tribes and became extinct in the past. To name some of them—the Andamanese and Rabaris of India, Nenets of Russia, Kolash of Pakistan, Maori of New Zealand etc. However, the situation today is completely different. This is an age of ethnic assertion, consciousness of language and culture, even to the extent of identity chauvinism and jingoism. The people are not only possessive of their ethnic identity but also zealously concerned for it. They are proud of their language, culture and past heritage. People go to the extent of resorting to violence in order to preserve, protect and develop their own culture, language and religion as it is happening in the North East India. They are totally bereft of the idea of co-existence, secularism and the spiritual ethics of "live and let live".

At such juncture, the Nepalis living in the North East India were yet the most cosmopolitan minded, accommodating and open to other's culture and language. Wherever they have settled down, be it hills or plains, they have adjusted themselves with the lifestyle of local tribe or community, adopted their language, dresses and culture and shared with their problems and prospects. Perhaps, it would not be exaggerated to say that, in the present context, the Nepalis in India are the only one community who adopt other's culture without a whimper and, at the same time, keep their own too. They are a community with sizeable population in Assam (5,64,790, Census 2001), have a rich and diverse culture and heritage and a language (Nepali) whose literature is sufficiently advanced that has found a place in the 8th Schedule of the Constitution of India. They want to live in Assam in complete harmony and brotherhood with the local people and at the same time preserve, protect and develop their own culture and language. They would like to identify themselves as Indian Nepalis or Gorkhas in exclusion of the Nepalese nationals from Nepal.

In Assam, they have fitted in well with the larger Assamese society consisting of Assamese, Boros, Rabhas, Kacharis, Garos, Koches etc. most of whom are their consanguinities (Kiratas). They have been here for the last two hundred years. They have forgotten their erstwhile country Nepal and lost all socio-political interest in it. Vast majority of them have even never been to Nepal. They have loved their new found land as their mother land, its surroundings, hills and valleys and the people who live here. They have adapted themselves well with the local people and their language and culture. They have also given their own culture and language to the people of this land, mostly the tribals of the hill states. In Khasi Hills, they lived for many years in cordial relations with the local inhabitants. Living together side by side for a long time they have mixed up their culture and language. The Nepalis spoke the Khasi language fluently and the Nepali womenfolk wore *jain kyrshah* (thin printed cotton clothe knotted at shoulder and covering the body up to foot) like Khasi women. They exchanged each others' culture and language. The Nepalis introduced the use of milk (drinking of milk with tea) among the Khasis for the first time, which they never did before. They also initiated a number of Nepali words into Khasi vocabulary which have become a part of the Khasi language today. The place names like Mahadewkhola, Dhankheti, Naspatighari, Nayabangla, Lalchanbasti etc. are all Nepali terms.

The people of the North East too found them to be simple, similar looking with themselves and *entente cordiale*. Hence they welcomed the Nepalis with their open heart. "They were largely well-accepted and well-treated in larger Assamese society"—was the comment of Manirul Hussain.[12] So they lived together, exchanged their cultures and traditions and at times, mixed their blood in legitimate matrimony, unlike many other communities who have come from outside and lived here for generations. Let me quote here, for example, from some writers about those outsiders living in Assam. Amalendu Guha writes:

> "In course of time the Nepalis became acultured with Assamese in respect of language, culture, tradition, but the Muslim immigrants remained as before

> even to this day. They even did not mix up with the Assamese Muslims who speak Assamese, follow Assamese culture, except profess Islam. Though they had common religion, the two communities are wide apart in culture, psychological make-up and socio-economic condition. Unlike the immigrant Muslims, their Assamese counterparts neither practised 'Purda' nor did they have professional zeal for Urdu as status symbol."[13]

Journalist, Shekhar Gupta writes about the Bengalis in Assam in his book entitled—"A Valley Divided":

> "There is no denying the fact that over the years Bengali cultural and linguistic arrogance has also contributed to this syndrome. The Bengali Hindu has by and large, refused to be identified with the Assamese. Even though he has made Assam his home he remains nostalgic about Calcutta. This attitude has made Bengalis unwelcome guests in all parts of the North East, be it Tripura, Assam, Meghalaya, Manipur or Nagaland."[14]

A colonial British officer has the following opinion about the Nepalis:

> "Though small in stature these Nepalis have big hearts—naturally vigorous, excitable and aggressive, they are very law abiding"—was the remark made by L.S.S.O'Malley, the author of the *Bengal District Gazetteers*.

Similarly, the Assamese were described by Col. Shakespear as—"a peaceful, almost effeminate race, in no great number, addicted, in large number, to opium eating and not disposed to diligent labour". So the two peoples made friends easily, lived together side by side in permanent peace and harmony. The Nepalis, wherever they lived, irrespective of hills or plains, spoke the local languages, dressed like the local people and acted in the manner their neighbours did, and merged in the Indian main stream, as the time passed by. Professor A.C. Sinha, noted Social scientist, remarked:

> "Most of the residents (Gorkhas) have adapted themselves to the local conditions in such a way that they are counted among the indigenous[15] people with all the benefits even though they have their own communities and their own way of life, speak their language and maintain their own tradition. But the Nepalis have a great capacity to assimilate themselves with the hill communities. They adopt the language of their neighbourhood, contract marital alliances and turn out to be an inseparable part of the local economy."[16]

The Nepalis participated in the local festivals and cultural activities of Assamese people like Bihu festival, Raslila, Sankar Dev/Madhab Dev Tithi, performance of Ankia Nat, Bhawana etc. Mention may be made of the active participation in Bihu festivals by Nepali artists like Anju Devi, Bipul Bahadur, Chandrakala Newar, Arati Pradhan, Gitanjali Chhetri etc.[17] Nepali young artist Raju Shrestha of Golaghat, Barapathar village excelled Assamese artists in Bihu dance and won prizes. He is also expert in Bihu song, Husari song and Bihunam and also plays Bihu Dhol and Pepa. Binod Khanal, another Nepali folk artiste received the Pratima Barua Pandey Memorial Award in December, 2018 for his excellent contribution to folk culture of Assam. This award which carried a citation and a cash prize of Rs. 25 thousand was sponsored by the All Assam Students Union (AASU) and was presented to him by AASU Adviser, Shri

Samujjal Kumar Bhattacharya.[18] Binod Khanal has dedicated 25 years of his life in development of Nepali and Assamese folk culture and worked in various theatres across Assam including Sonam Theatre, Axomi Theatre, Bhaskar Theatre, Nataraj Theatre, Aradhana Theatre, Brahmaputra Theatre etc. Nepali youths regularly take part in the cultural shows during the Asom Sahitya Sabha Sessions. Greeting of near and dear ones with *fulam-gamosa*, usage of *Kharudaiya Japi* in the working field, entertaining guests with *Tamol-Pan Bota* or *Kharai* and wearing *Eri-chadar* in winter cold are common practices of the Nepalis in Assam. The Nepali women folk wear *Riha-mekhela chadar* while attending social function. They also join Assamese women in catching fish in the *Khal-bil* with Jakoi. Majgaon and Bahbari, two closely situated villages inhabited by Nepali and Asamiya communities since 150 years past have exhibited an exemplary assimilation of mutual cultures and languages. Assamese girls like Dipika Goswami, Dikshyamani Das and Pabitra Bhuyan of Bahbari village have earned accolades by singing beautiful Nepali songs while Nepali youths like Hemanta Timsina, Samir Pokhrel and many others of Majgaon have shown their talents by participating in Ras-Bhawna and Assamese cultural shows. In Gangmouthan (near Behali) the holy *Than* of Mahapurukh Sankardev is deeply revered by the Nepalis of that locality. One Raghubir Chhetri renovated the *Than* by removing the decayed and shrivelled thatch roof with GCI sheet. Besides taking care of the *Than,* one Nepali Brahmin offers prayers to it every day.[19] This reminds us of one Nepali Brahmin, Rati Kanta Upadhyaya by name who acted as *Satradhikar* of two *Satras*, one at Tiyak of Sibsagar and another at Nowgong which are known as *Nepali Satras* till today. This Nepali Brahmin Rati Kanta Upadhyaya so fully assimilated with Assamese culture that, Dr. Tirthanath Sarma was led to presume that the present host of Assamese *Gokhains* might be the descendants of this Nepali *Satradhikar*.

Closely following the footsteps of Rati Kanta Upadhyaya, as discussed above, another devoted Nepali, Mohanlal Upadhyaya played a significant role in propagation of Neo-Vaishnavism of Srimanta Sankar Dev. He was a dedicated Bhakta of Mahapurus Shrimanta Sankar Dev and an active member of the Sankar Sangha from 1947 to 1970. With a view to propagating Sankardev's mission he founded his own Sangha in 1971 known as Sri Sri Sankardeb Prachar Sangha and took upon himself the leadership of the Sangha as its President. He preached the teachings of Sri Sankardev among the people tirelessly travelling from place to place across the state of Assam. He indoctrinated thousands of people of various communities including Nepali and established many *Namghars* in Dhemaji, Lakhimpur, Biswanath, Sonitpur, Golaghat, Morigaon, Nagaon, Karbi Anglonbg, Chaigaon etc. The Asom Sahitya Sabha published a booklet entitled "Asamiya Nepali Samaj Aru Sanskritir Ruprekha" in which Mohanlal Upadhyaya was described as "a whole hearted devotee of Mahapurush Srimanta Sankardev". He steered by himself the Sri Sri Sankardev Prachar Sangha as its President for 48 years, from its founding till his death in August, 2018. At present the Sangha is run by a committee of three members one of which is the son of Mohanlal Upadhyaya himself (*History and Culture of Assamese Nepali*, Government of Assam, pp. 397-98).

Impact of Assamese Language on Nepalis

The children of Nepalis in Assam do not go to Nepali medium schools. They study in Assamese medium schools right from Pre-primary standard to Matriculation. Except a few schools in Shillong, Gauhati, Tura and Dibrugarh there is no Nepali medium school in the whole of Brahmaputra valley of Assam. Unlike other communities such as Bengalis, Biharis and Muslims, the Nepali guardians of Assam have never felt the necessity of sending their children to Nepali medium school. They value Assamese language even more than many of the Asamiyas who send their wards to English medium schools. The children of Nepalis not only communicate in Assamese language but also write letters to their parents and friends in Assamese language, because they do not know how to write in Nepali script. This fact has not pinched the guardians a little or prompted them to establish Nepali schools for their children. It is not that they have no money to construct and maintain Nepali school: they have constructed many Assamese schools and colleges for their children and donated generously to such schools. For example, in 1941 Chabilal Upadhyaya established Behali High School in the Nepali concentrated area which is running till today but he never asked for introducing Nepali medium in that school. Devi Prasad Pokhrel donated Rs. 40,000 to Behali High School, Brihaspati Upadhyaya donated Rs. 20,000 to Hari Mandir, Prabhuram Karki donated Rs. 5,000 to Darrang College and Prasad Singh Subba donated his land to Netra Milon Chhetra. A number of educational institutions were built up in various parts of Assam with the financial help and efforts of Nepalis like, Bhim Bahadur Vidyapith (MV School), Buda Chapari M.E. School, Behali MV School, Prajapati Rijal Higher Secondary School, Gamiri, Shingari, Nikasi, Sholong, Lekhapani, Purbanchal High School etc. The hard earned money of these Nepalis by selling milk and paddy, jute and sugarcane etc. go for the construction of Assamese school buildings with a sense of missionary zeal and enthusiasm.

The palpable result of this philanthropic tasks of these broad minded Nepalis of Assam, was the emergence of a large scale pro-Asamiya Nepali educated youths who were the future builders of Assam. There cropped up a good number of Nepali youths educated in Assamese schools who become doctors, engineers, lawyers, professors etc. and they turned out to be the proud assets and future builders of Assam. The Assamese language became the common medium of expression which so permeated into the daily conversation among the Nepalis that many Assamese words crept into Nepali colloquial vocabulary. A few of them are given below.

Nepali	Assamese	Corrupted Nepali
Kera	Kal	Kol
Bhui Katar	Anaras	Anaras
Ukhu	Kuhiyar	Kuier
Inar/Kup	Kuwa	Kuwa
Dailo	Darja	Darja
Jhyal	Khiriki	Khirki
Pul	Dalang	Dolong
Dunga	Naw	Naw
Supari	Tamol	Tamal
Chiya	Shah	Cha
Besar	Haladi	Haldi
Kaag	Kauri	Kaurhi
Utranu	Namaa	Namnu
Charhnu	Uthaa	Uthnu
Piunu	Khowa	Khanu

NOTES

1. B.N. Luniya (1998). *Evolution of Indian Culture,* p. 221.
2. Edward Gait (1992). *A History of Assam,* (*reprint*), p. 7.
3. *Ibid.*, p. 11.
4. Kanak Lal Baruah (2002). "Early History of Kamrupa, 1933". In *Ethnicity and Cross-border Movements in the North East: A Study of the Nepalis in Assam,* Lopita Nath, p. 58.

5. Bishnulal Upadhyaya (2004). *Khanmihali* (in Assamese), Sonitpur Printers, Tezpur, p. 32.
6. A.C. Sinha (2003). "Indian North East Frontier and Nepali Immigrants". In *The Nepalis in The North East,* A.C. Sinha and T.B. Subba (eds.), Indus Publishing Co., New Delhi, p. 52.
7. *Ibid.*, p. 36.
8. Khemraj Sharma (2013). *Gorkhas in the Wilderness,* Concept Publishing Company Pvt. Ltd., New Dwlhi, p.103.
9. Dr. Hutton, *Studies in Early History of Assam.*
10. Edward Gait (1905). *A History of Assam,* p. 16.
11. Manirul Hussain (1993). *The Assam Movement,* Manak Publication, New Delhi, p. 255.
12. *Ibid.*, p. 260.
13. Amalendu Guha (2006). *Planters Raj to Swaraj,* p. 170.
14. Sekhar Gupta (1984). *A Valley Divided,* Vikash Publishing House, New Delhi, p. 129.
15. Bishnulal Upadhyaya (2004). *Khanmihali* (in Assamese), Tezpur, p. 40.
16. A.C. Sinha (1990). "The Indian North East Frontier and Nepali Immigrants". In *Himalayan Environment and Culture,* N.K. Rustomji and Charles Ramble (eds.), New Delhi, p. 236.
17. Bishnulal Upadhyaya (2004). *Khanmihali,* Tezpur.
18. Sentinel, dated 28 December, 2018.
19. *Ibid.*, p. 39.

2

The Nepalis in Assam

It is more than two hundred years now that the Nepalese or Gorkhas had first come to India as recruits in the Indian army. While the primary reason for their coming to India may be ascribed to be for earning their livelihood, it was, rather the motivation of British Government which largely prompted the Gorkhas to cross over into India. From the discussions to be followed in this chapter, it will appear that the Nepalese were, by and large, imported by the British for their benefit rather than they came on their own initiative. The Gorkha recruitment in the Indian army started from 1815, a year before the signing of the ignominious treaty of Segowlee between Nepal Durbar and the East India Company. While the Anglo-Nepal war was still in its peak and Major Gabriel Martindel was fighting at Nalapani where General Gillespie's detachment was vanquished by the Gorkhas, Lieutenant Frederik Young hurriedly raised an irregular Gorkha force of 4500 strong drawn from the prisoner of war camps in Dehradun, Nahan and Sirmur. Two palpable reasons have been put forward by the historians for this act of headlong Gorkha recruitment by the British.

Firstly, the British Generals were highly impressed by the extreme bravery and elan demonstrated by the Nepalese soldiers in the Indo-Nepal war. From the experience they gathered in the past through working with their own Indian native sepoys they could discover in the Gorkhas the right material that they had been looking for—that was, their bravery and total absence of fear for death. David Ochterlony, the British General who conducted the Anglo-Nepal war said—"The Indian soldiers of the Company would never be able to hold their own against the Nepalese in their mountain fastness". Sir Charles Metcalf, a British army Commander ruefully remarked—"We have met with an enemy who shows decidedly greater bravery and greater steadiness than our troops possess. Our troops have been beaten by the enemy; *Khukris* in hand driven miles like a flock of sheep". Thus, it was Sir David Octerlony himself who originated the idea of enlisting Gorkhas in the Company's army and vigorously pursuing the policy for implementation.

Secondly, apart from the fighting qualities of the Gorkhas other political considerations were no less important to motivate the East India Company to recruit the Gorkhas in their Indian army. The British was quick to recognize the turbulent population of Nepal, well trained in warfare and itching for war and plunder, and restive for territorial expansion, like a heap of explosives waiting ignition. This was a danger signal for the British. Even if Nepal herself remained non-aggressive, there were many Indian Native Rajas who could easily utilize Nepalese military power against the British. Moreover, Nepal had a close relations and cultural affinities with India, besides family ties with many Indian princes through marriages which could lead to political alliance against the British at any time. B.H.Hodgson, the British Resident in Nepal, even strongly suspected Bhimsen Thapa, the Prime Minister of Nepal's policy of building military strength to use it against the British at an opportune time. Hodgson was confident that security of British India rested on the weakening of military strength of Nepal and that could be possible only by draining out the young population of Nepal through their recruitment in Indian army. The Gorkha soldiers recruited in India, at the same time, Hodgson pleaded, could be held as pledges for Nepal's good behaviour during any belligerency if so occur with Nepal. These were some of the impelling and crucial diplomatic considerations which prompted the East India Company to rush with the process of Gorkha recruitment.

At the initial stage the recruitment of Gorkhas in British army was not an easy task. The Durbar of Nepal was against the idea of their subjects joining the British army. Nepal strictly followed a close-door policy and did not allow any foreigner to enter the country. In spite of this situation, the East India Company continued recruitment by clandestinely enticing Gorkha youths from Nepal through the help of secret agents. The British recruiting agencies adopted all means of foul practices to meet the ever increasing demand for Gorkha recruits. This practice of clandestine recruitment continued till 1884 when an agreement of Mutual Concession was signed under which a limited number of Gorkha recruits were allowed by Nepali Prime Minister Rannupdip Singh on exchange of British manufactured arms and ammunitions. After this the restriction on recruitment became gradually liberal and the East India Company enhanced its policy of Gorkha recruitment. The Ist World War required enormous manpower for reinforcement of Indian army for which Chandra Samsher Rana opened up Nepal's doors for Gorkha recruitment to the British Government. The result was astounding; during the period of war 2,00,000 of Nepal's best young men were brought into the roll of the Indian army.[1] It is said that Nepal's agricultural operations came to grinding halt for a few years due to want of workers. During the Second World War too Gorkha recruitment was so colossal that the twenty battalions of Gorkha Rifles of the Ist World War were expanded to forty-five during the Second World War period. Due to coercive policy adopted by the recruiting authorities, a large number of Gorkha young men fled Nepal and entered Assam, Darjeeling and Sikkim in order to avoid compulsory army recruitment.

In Assam, the Gorkha soldiers were deployed for the first time in 1817 during the wake of Burmese invasion. The British deputed the Cuttack Legion (later changed the name to Sylhet Light Infantry) which consisted of 1,000 Gorkha and Hindustani soldiers to Assam in order to check the Burmese invasion. The Gorkha soldiers were, finally instrumental in driving away the Burmese from Assam and rescuing Assamese people from the barbaric aggression of the Burmese. It was a time when the Ahom rule was in a state of doldrum; the royal court had become a hot-bed of conspiracies involving internal squabbles, murder and rivalry among the royal princes. Taking the advantage of political turmoil, the Burmese overran the country unleashing a reign of terror, with barbaric plunder, kidnapping and murder. "Thirty thousand Assamese had been carried off as slaves by the Burmese. Many thousands had lost their lives and large tracts of country been laid desolate by the wars, famines and pestilences."[2] Assam, in the words of Anandaram Dhekial Phukan (1829–1859), "groaned under the oppression and lawless tyranny of the Burmese", that destroyed more than half of the Assamese population, and those who survived had almost given up cultivation and lived chiefly on jungle roots and plants.[3] In 1826, the British troops completely expelled the Burmese from the Brahmaputra valley, and quelled the Moamoriah rebellion.

Manipur was restored back to Gambhir Singh, the Jaintia Raja, Ram Singh, was confirmed in his possessions both in the hills and the plain belts of Surma valley and Govind Chandra was reinstated as the Raja of Cachar. Historian H.K. Borpujari termed this act of the British East India Company as "divine dispensation", meaning as blessings of God.

Gorkha Settlement in Assam

After retirement, the British Government encouraged the Gorkha ex-servicemen to settle down in the places of their posting by providing them with land, jobs and other economic opportunities. They were employed in the government civil offices as Peons, Choukidars and Chaprasis. Their sincerity and loyalty earned them job opportunities in private companies, tea gardens, coal mines and many other institutions. The Assam Rifles rehabilitated its Gorkha ex-servicemen on at least forty Headquarters, such as—Sadiya, Guwahati and Nowgong in Assam, Shillong in Khasi Hills, Mantripokhari in Manipur, Aizawl in Mizoram and Mokokchung in Nagaland, Tura in Garo Hills etc. All these places became the nucleus for the growth of Gorkha community. Side by side with the para-military forces, the government maintained a large number of regular Gorkha regiments with their Headquarters in different places of the North East, like Shillong, Guwahati, Tura, Jorhat, Dibrugarh, Kohima, Aijawal, Agartala etc. It was the principle of the British Government to look after the well-being of the family members of the Indian army, as the British believed, that would indirectly account for their efficiency. In 1864, the government introduced Regimental homes to accommodate families of the Gorkha soldiers in all the important Headquarters of Gorkha regiments. Around these Regimental Homes all types of basic amenities like schools for children, hospitals, clubs, markets were made available to them. These centres popularly came to be known as Gorkha villages. In Shillong, for example, the Gorkha Regimental Home was established in 1891 at Jhalupara (Shillong) in order to provide accommodation to the families of Gorkha soldiers. That is why Jhalupara and Mawprem are Gorkha concentration centres in Shillong till today. The government encouraged the Gorkha soldiers to bring their families from Nepal even by giving them travel expenses so that their offsprings would meet the requirement of future recruits, and the government would not have to depend on Nepal for supply of Gorkha recruits. Because British need for Gorkha recruits was great while their supply was meager. Therefore in order to attract Gorkhas to settle down in Assam lands were freely settled to Gorkha ex-servicemen in the vicinity of the Regimental Homes. Captain Francis Jenkins in his report of 1832 recommended that instead of pensions, the ex-servicemen of the local corps should be given grant of land.[4] The Gorkhas who retired from service and wanted to settle down in Assam gladly accepted this offer of Captain Jenkins. Apart from the coming of Gorkha recruits, a large number of civilian Nepalese found their ways into Assam in successive waves in search of greener pasture. They were more than happy to settle down in the Brahmaputra Valley and in the hill districts of the North East and eke out their living by doing cultivation work, dairy farming, serving as office Peons, Choukidars and doing many other odd jobs.

After assumption of governance of Assam, the next imperative before the British was to rejuvenate the devastated economy of Assam through development of agriculture. David Scott, Agent to the Governor General and Commissioner of Revenue in Assam had been instrumental in building up the structure of revenue administration in Assam since 1824 when the British first occupied this part of the North-eastern Frontiers.

Gorkhas or Nepalis?

To an Indian the two terms Gorkha and Nepalis are confusing and difficult to make out who is a Gorkha or a Nepali. In Indian context both the terms are interexchangable and needs to be explained. The Nepalis are not one community but a heterogenous amalgam of many communities like the Brahmins (Bahuns) Chhetris, Newars, Rais, Limbus, Magars, Tamangs, Gurungs, Sherpas etc. They have their own specific languages, cultures and religions. There are 123 number of languages spoken in Nepal. However, in India they are considered as one community called Gorkha or Nepalis with one Nepali language spoken by all. They all look the same and speak same Nepali language. In this book I have used these two terms indiscriminately according to the situations. But in Nepal, the term "Gorkha is used in a restricted sense while the term 'Nepali' connotes the inhabitants of the country." In other word "Gorkha" may be conjured up historically as the country or kingdom of Prithvinarayan Shah while "Nepali" stands for the nationality. The term Gorkha is used on more official and specific purposes than Nepali, such as "Gorkha Raj", "Gorkha Patra", "Gorkha Muluk", "Gorkha Palton" etc. To understand the meaning of the term "Gorkha" more clearly, we have to go to the root from where the word was coined. The word Gorkha has emerged from the root name "Go-ra-kh", the abbreviation of Gorakhnath, the Patron Saint of the principality called Gorkha, that was located on the west of Kathmandu. Prithvinarayan Shah, the king of Gorkha who is credited to have unified present Nepal in the 18th century, was from this Gorkha Principality. He was known as the Gorkha king and his army which conquered the whole of Nepal was known as Gorkha Palton. It was the same Gorkhali force which fought against the British in the Anglo-Nepal war of 1814-16 under the leadership of General

Amarsingh Thapa and earned the praise of the British. These Gorkhas were recruited in the Indian army by the British since 1815 and their regiment were named as Gorkha Rifles. The Gorkhas are serving as such in the Indian army ever since than till today. The Indian Gorkhas living in different parts of India are the descendants of the Gorkha soldiers who served as British soldiers and settled down permanently in India after retirement and died in India. This is the reason why the Indian Nepalis like to be called themselves as Gorkhas. Subhas Ghising, the supremo of the Gorkha National Liberation Front (GNLF) is of the opinion that "Gorkha" should replace the name "Nepali". He even asked all the people who called themselves as Nepalis to leave Darjeeling and go to Nepal (Subba, 2003: 200). The word "Nepali", according to him, meant a Nepali national and hence should go to Nepal. Ever since that time the controversy whether Indian Nepalis should be called Nepalis or Gorkhas or Gorkhalis has persisted among the Indian Nepalis without any solution.

After having lived in India for generations, the heterogenous Nepal's communities forgot their mother tongue and started speaking in Nepali language. The Nepali language became the lingua-franca of the Nepalis in India and contributed to the unification of the Indian Nepalis into one homogeneous socio-cultural and political group of *Nepali Jati*. It made them feel as one Indian Nepali nationality, transcending their caste distinction that separated them while in Nepal. In Nepal if a person is asked about his identity, the answer will be definitely —a Newar or Rai or Limbu, Gurung, Magar, so on and so forth. But when that person comes to India, he forgets about his ethnic identity and becomes a generic Nepali. Professor T.B. Subba writes—"Thus, it is the etic situation that brings a large number of historically, racially, culturally, linguistically and religiously divergent groups under a common identity called

'Nepali' or 'Gorkha'. Whether he is a Bahun or a Kami makes no difference to a Naga as it does not matter whether he is an Ao or Sema to a Nepali."[5] The social barrier of casteism that plagued Nepal was broken down in Assam. For the Nepalis in India the centuries old caste ridden history of Nepal is a closed book. In India they became Indian Nepalis or Gorkhas and the Nepali language, became their lingua-franca. The acceptance of Nepali language as lingua-franca in all parts of India by various ethnic groups like Rai, Limbu, Gurung, Tamang, Newar, Sunuwar, Thami, Sherpa, Lepcha etc. made them feel as belonging to one group, one *Jati* and one nationality. That is the identity that the Nepalis living in India are trying hard to bring home before the Indian people, today.

Impact of Alien Culture

The geography, climate and the social environment of a country always exercise a great impact on the pattern of socio-cultural life of the people. They go a long way to mould the character, lifestyle and the livelihood pattern of the people. The Nepalis of the North East were no exception to this universal rule. Living in Assam for long period with the new people and alien culture they could no longer hold on to their own. In the new place and new order of things their systems seemed to be outlandish; their dresses and wearing apparels looked grotesque in the eyes of local people. One by one, they became obsolete and disused. Gradually, the Nepalis came under the influence of new culture, alien language and their lifestyle. They tried to hold on to their own as long as they could, but as the time passed, their systems seemed to be not conforming to the new environment or their traditional articles made in Nepal became not easily available in Assam. The new generations of Indian Nepalis gradually forgot their folk tales (*Katha-kuthungri*), folk song (*Lok Geet*), adages

(*Akhyan*), parables (*Tukka-kissa*), riddles (*Gaukhane Katha*), and all forms of superstitions like (*Jaadu-Tuna, Tantra-Mantra, Bokshi-Daini, Jhakri-Dhami*) etc. These all became the order of the past. Some of the cultures, for example—the tradition of *Bhat-Kharao jaane, Khadoh jagaune, silok gaune* and *Ratewli Khelne* that used to be the integral features of Nepali marriage ceremony in the past are no longer practiced anywhere in Assam. Well enough, they celebrate *Dasain* (Durga Puza) but they don't know how to sing *Malshri, a* beautiful piece of Nepali classical music. *Deushi, Bhailo/Bhaileni* are performed here and there today by some Nepali boys and girls but the lyric and traditional tune are totally lost. *Naumati Baja* that used to be an inseparable part of Nepali marriage ceremony has now been replaced by the blare of film song which goes well with new generation Nepali youths.

Impact on Language

As the Nepalis lived together with their local neighbours, in close social relationship for generations their children learnt the local languages and adopted their cultures which gradually impacted their own Nepali language. Altough they continued to speak Nepali many words from local language crept into their colloquial Nepali tongue. These alien words, in course of time, came to be used as Nepali words without their knowledge. Today, the Nepalis living in different states of the North East, speak degenerated colloquial Nepali language although their written Nepali language is still in tact. Some samples of these corrupted Nepali words are produced below:

Nepali	Corrupted Nepali	Nepali	Corrupted Nepali
Ukhu	Kuier	Kera	Kol
Chia	Cha	Tato	Garam
Chiso	Thanda	Utranu	Namnu
Chadnu	Uthnu	Guwa	Tamul
Dhoka	Darja	Sadak	Rasta
Sancho	Tala	Tankha	Betan
Inar	Kuwa	Machis	Salai
Bijan	Guti	Khudkilo	Jakhala
Tagaro	Nangla	Kucho	Jaru
Chiya	Piunu	Chaa	Khanu
Okhati	Dabai	Chhito	Jaldi

The fact of the matter is that, culture does not remain static. It changes with the process of human development. Culture also mixes up with another culture when two different peoples live together or a completely new culture is born in the process. The former is called "Cultural Syncretism" and the latter is called the "Process of Synthesis" in Anthropological terms. Indian culture is the assimilation and synthesization of many cultures of the Aryans, Mongolians, Persians, Sakas, Hunas, Mughals etc. during the long process of history. The same thing happened to Nepali culture. They too settled down permanently in the North East, mixed up their culture and language with the local people, leading to cultural syncretisation; something they lost, some other thing they gained and the *vice-versa*.

With the human development and change of time our thoughts and belief system have compelled us to change our culture, customs and manner. For example, today our children must go to school at four years of age, a pregnant woman must go to hospital to deliver a baby, she must undergo pre-natal and post-natal course of medical treatment. The system of polygamy, child marriage, *sati pratha* which prevailed in old culture have now become the order of the past. These are a few instances, among many, which once formed a part of our culture have now been given a go-bye.

Livelihood and Occupation

In Assam the land was plenty whereas population was thin making the agricultural prospect promising. But the local Assamese, people were given to opium addiction and totally uninterested to work. They would rather love to cultivate opium for their home consumption. So the British Government was looking for people from outside Assam who were interested to come to Assam to carry out cultivation. The retired Gorkhas who had settled down in Assam were found to be good in cultivation and also diligent and hard working people. Hence, the Government encouraged them by giving as much land as they could put to use. David Scott, the Political Agent to the Governor in Council, authorized Captain Neufville to grant his Gorkhas who had brought their families with them, lands at a very moderate rate of eight *Annas* per *Pura* annually. The Gorkhas took full advantage of this concessional offer of land. Immigration of Nepalis was not only due to encouragement of the British but also welcomed by Assamese intelligentsia. Anandoram Dhekial Phukan (1827–1859) commented "—more than one-half of the country is now a vast extant of waste" and, he opined that Government should bring experienced people from outside for increasing food production. Gunaviram Barua (1834–1894) estimated that no less than a million people from outside could easily be settled on the wide areas of Assam. He enumerated three factors which were favourable to such immigration. These were—(1) Cheapness and fertility of the land, (2) Attractive earning from skilled labour and craftsman in view of the local manpower shortage, and (3) the prevailing condition of easy matrimony into local families."[6] In a letter addressed to A.J.M. Mills in 1853 Major H. Vetch, the Deputy Commissioner wrote—"In a country so abounding with wasteland as Assam and with so scanty a population, Government may well part with a portion on any term, if thereby settlers be induced to come into the country."[7] Therefore, lands were freely settled to Gorkha ex-servicemen in the vicinity of the Regimental Homes as well as civilian Gorkhas who came from Nepal to settle down. Needless to say, collection of land revenue was one of the main objectives of British agrarian policy. For this purpose, the land was classified into different categories in 1868-69 and different rates of land revenue were imposed.[8]

The migration of Gorkhas from Nepal increased and very soon the hard working Gorkha peasants were able to double the food production against the soaring demand. They brought more land under cultivation and engaged additional men and materials into cultivation. Dr. A. Guha writes:

> "Increase of tea garden labourers pushed the demand for food. To meet this demand, Nepalis agriculture got boosted up. With the increase in population the demand for food grains increased. Government encouraged increase of agricultural activities by importing Nepalis and settling them in Assam."[9]

The enterprising Gorkhas cultivated different crops such as paddy, mustard seed, jute, sugar cane, pulses and various kinds of vegetables, and fruits throughout the year, from season to season. Betel-nut, *pan* leave and fruits used to be grown in their backyard which also brought them extra income without putting additional work. They also reared other live-stocks, such as goats, pigs and poultry for which the daily kitchen wastes were sufficient feed. Sugarcane was the main crop grown by the Gorkhas of Darrang, Lakhimpur and Sibsagar districts where large areas of land were brought under this cultivation. The Gorkhas became rich very soon, converted their thatched houses into Assam type houses with GCI sheet roofs. Many of them saved their money by buying gold and silver, for banking system was not known to them. Gorkha women covered their bodies with gold ornaments from head to toe and became the most ornamentally dressed women.

British Agrarian Policy

After the assumption of power, the Government of India turned out to be not merely an administrator but also a "Chief landlord". The entire land covered under the Brahmaputra valley and the Surma valley belonged to the Government. Efficient land administration and proper utilization of land resource for increased agricultural production and development of economy was the primary desideratum of the Government. The old Ahom system of "Khel and Got" was replaced by new land revenue and administration rules. The Government introduced a series of land laws during the span of 1854 to 1893 that included, the promulgation of Assam Land and Revenue Regulations, 1886, Cadastral Survey Operations in 1883-93, land settlement rules, assessment and levy of land revenue rules etc. The Government of India also separated Assam from Bengal and upgraded Assam into Chief Commissioners Province in 1874.

Collection of land revenue was one of the main objectives of British agrarian policy. For this purpose, the land was classified into different categories in 1868-69. The peasants were taxed on their landed property, products and transports. Initially poll tax of three rupees per head was levied in upper Assam. In the Lower and Central Assam, a tax of two rupees was imposed on Paiks for which they were entitled to two *Puras* of land each.[10] For the purpose of levying land revenue, the land was classified into three categories. The most fertile cultivable land where winter crop or transplanted paddy is grown was called *Rupit,* the dry weather crop land was termed as *Faringati* and the homestead land or garden land were known as *Basti.* The rates of revenue for the above different categories lands were fixed and re-fixed from time to time according to changing conditions. Initially, the average rates of land revenue in the Brahmaputra valley were 6 annas per bigha for Basti land, 5 annas per bigha for Rupit and 4 annas per bigha for Faringati. In 1861, Colonel Hopkinson put forward a proposal to increase the rates of land revenue and accordingly the rates were arbitrarily raised to double in 1867. Table 2.1 shows the enhanced rates of revenue fixed by Government from the year 1868-69.

Table 2.1: Land revenue assessment on different Categories of Land in 1868-69; per Bigha

District	Rupit	Faringati	Basti
Kamrup	10 Annas	8 Annas	1 Rupee
Darrang	10 Annas	8 Annas	1 Rupee
Nowgong	10 Annas	8 Annas	1 Rupee
Sibsagar	10 Annas	8 Annas	1 Rupee
Lakhimpur	10 Annas	8 Annas	1 Rupee

Source: Barpujari, *op cit.* (1993), p. 35.

As a result of these enhanced rates, the revenue income of the Government jumped from Rs. 10,01,733 in 1864 to Rs. 21,65,157 in 1872-73. In 1889, the Government of India conducted another reassessment of land revenue and further increased the rates of land revenue from the year 1893. This resulted in the increase of additional revenue income of Rs. 1,10,000 annually, which was equivalent to an increase of 33 per cent on the figure of previous year. In 1893-94, the

Government further classified each of the three categories of land into three grades according to quality and revised the land revenue as shown in the Table 2.2.

Table 2.2: Land Revenue rates as finally fixed in 1893-94

Classes of land	Rates proposed per Bigha		
	Rs.	**Annas**	**Paisa**
1. Domestic or garden land			
1st class	1	6	0
2nd class	1	4	0
3rd class	1	2	0
2. Rupit land			
1st class	1	0	0
2nd class	0	14	0
3rd class	0	12	0
3. Faringati			
1st class	0	14	0
2nd clas	0	10	0
3rd class	0	9	0

Source: Barpujari, *op cit.,* p. 36.

But, in spite of the systematic revenue maximization, nothing was done by the Government to improve the condition of agriculture in Assam. No attempt was made to deal with the recurring floods and the few embankments that were built were nothing but makeshift arrangements. The cultivators of Assam reeled under heavy assessment as mentioned above. As the time passed by, criticisms and objections were raised by the *Raijmels* (Farmers, organizations) and elite Assamese people against the high rates of land revenue imposed on the poor farmers.

When British Government failed to respond to the popular resentment of mass people, Maniram Dewan and Anandaram

Dhekial Phukan submitted memorandum to Government. The loyal Nepalis, however, had nothing to complaint against, for according to them *Sarkari Khajana* must be given to the king. But the Assamese ryots were determined not to yield to Gorvement. They convened Mels and Raijmels for the redressal of their grievances. Finally, the peoples' resentment found expression in the Phulaguri uprising in 1961, the first instance of organized resistance through the institution of Raijmel. Despite the repressive measures adopted by the Government to quell the uprising, the ryots continued to protest vehemently against the high rates of land revenue until they succeeded. The Government was compelled to lower the land revenue rates, first to 53 per cent and subsequently to 32.7 per cent.

The Government revised and reformed the land laws. The decennial landholders who paid land revenue directly to Government under the Assam Land and Revenue Regulations 1886, were, for the first time, defined in legal terms as the Ryots who enjoyed permanent, heritable and transferable right of use and occupancy in their lands. In the case of annual settlements, the existing practice was allowed to continue. For collection of land revenue Mouzadars were appointed who also acted as the executants of the District Collectors' orders. The Mouzadars were paid commissions on percentage basis on the total collection of revenue made by them annually. For proper administration, a Mouza area was divided into several Mandal areas, each containing not less than two hundred houses and entrusted to a Mandal whose function was to help the Mouzadar in keeping records about transfer of land ownership by death or sale, changes of land areas etc. in the Chitha/Jamabandi registers. In every village there used to be appointed a village Headman called Goanburah who helped the Mandal and Mouzadar in all types of village level *sarkari* matters. For the purpose of development of agriculture with better administration, the Government created the Department of Agriculture, Revenue and Commerce in 1870 as per the recommendation of the Finance Commission of 1866.

The Government of Assam attached great importance to agriculture as it earned land revenue for them by bringing more land under tillage, besides increasing food production for the growing population. Large areas of land were allotted to farmers who reclaimed them and brought under cultivation. People of Nepalese origin were encouraged to come to Assam even providing them onward journey expenses.[11] They were liberally given settlement of waste lands which resulted in large scale destruction and denudation of forest. Mention may be made that David Scott, the Political Agent to the Governor in Council, authorized Captain Neufville to grant his Gorkhas who had brought their families with them, lands at a very moderate rate of eight Annas per *pura* annually. The Gorkhas took full advantage of this concessional offer of land.

The success stories in agriculture attained by the forerunner Nepalis who came to Assam earlier, provided strong motivation to others in Nepal to come and take to agriculture. They found the soil of Assam very fertile and temperate climate suitable for cultivation of a wide varieties of crops. Plenty of land and easy to get settlement provided them further incentive. "Any unoccupied waste land could be taken up for cultivation without notice or application, and when so taken up, was settled with the occupant.[12] The enterprising Nepali farmers who had never possessed a shred of land in Nepal could hardly resist the lure of owning large tracts of land in Assam. The idea of getting away from the age-old bondage of tenancy and oppression in Nepal and becoming proud owner of land in Assam greatly incited the Nepalis. They started crossing over the border without any hindrance. The presence of various environmental hurdles and logistic constraints of the place did not deter them as their strong will to work hard and ubiquitous *khukuri* were by their side to avert any difficulty. They would clear large forests, level down the hills, confront wild animals and withstand the fear of malaria and black-fever. They would confront any problem in Assam rather than working as bonded farmer under the feudal landlords, the legacy that came down to them from their forebears who were tenant farmers for generations in Nepal. Initially, they came to Assam accompanied with relatives or known person and after having settled down and worked for a few years they brought their families too.

A joint report on Assam by Captain Francis Jenkins and Lieutenant Robert Pemberton of 1832 recommended that instead of pensions, the ex-servicemen of the local corps should be given grant of land. The report further stated[13]:

> "An increase to our cultivation and villages is beyond all doubt of the greatest importance to the present as well as future prosperity of this barren province, and might be accomplished by admitting monied speculating foreigners to hold lands on a long lease and encouraging Manipuries and Gurkhas and others who may feel inclined to colonise for the inhabitants are by no means prolific."

The Gorkhas who retired from service and wanted to settle down in Assam gladly accepted this suggestion of Captain Jenkins. This policy of the government led to the growth of large concentrations of Gorkha communities at various centres across North East. As the immigration of Nepalis gained momentum, more and more land came under tillage and the revenue for the Government multiplied. The land area possessed by Nepali immigrants increased exponentially from 17,000 acres in 1913-14 to 28,000 acres in 1919-20, in the Brahmaputra valley. The Nepalis population in three districts of Brahmaputra valley as shown in Table 2.3 increased significantly.

Table 2.3: Increase in number of Nepali immigrants

Districts	1921	1931
Darrang	18,997	24,862
Kamrup	8,527	10,101
Lakhimpur	8,440	11,951
Total	**35,964**	**46,914**

Source: Census of India, 1931, Vol. III, Assam, p. 53.

In Darrang, Lakhimpur and Sibsagar districts sugarcane cultivation was the main crop grown by the Nepalis and large areas were brought under this cultivation. The Nepalis concentrated in these areas setting up villages, some of them were named as Kuherbari (Kuher means sugarcane + bari means farm).They became rich very soon, converted their thatch houses into Assam type houses with GCI sheet roofs. Many of them saved their money by buying gold and silver, for banking system was not known to them. Nepali women covered their bodies from head to foot with gold ornaments and earned the name for the community. Table 2.4 shows the cultivated areas in the prominent districts of Assam during the initial period of agricultural growth in Assam.

Table 2.4: Total cultivated acreage in Assam proper

Districts	Cultivated acreage in 1849-50	Cultivated acreage in 1852-53
Kamrup	4,72,624	4,78,699
Darrang	2,33,615	2,23,699
Nowgong	1,81,917	1,74,777
Sibsagar	1,68,164	1,80,673
Lakhimpur	21,234	21,483
Total	**10,77,554**	**10,79,331**

Source: Mills Report on the Province of Assam (66) 5 and Appendix A.

Table 2.5 gives us district-wise population of the Assam valley for the years 1826, 1835 and 1872.

Table 2.5: Total population of Assam proper

District	1826	1835	1872
Kamrup	3,00,000	3,87,775	5,61,681
Darrang	89,519	1,85,569	2,35,720
Nowgong	90,000	2,41,300	2,60,238
Sibsagar	-	1,59,573	3,17,799
Lakhimpur	2,50,000	85,296	1,21,267
Total	**7 to 8 lacs**	**10,59,513**	**14,96,705**

Source: Mills Report, 1854 (66) App AI.

The flow of Nepalese immigrants into Assam ever continued resulting in increase in the area of cultivation. The total land area occupied and cultivated by Nepalese in 1939-40 rose to 1,04,773 acres*, within Assam valley only. Simultaneously, their population increased from 88,306 in 1931 to 1,01,338 in 1951, (as per Assam census reports, 1951). Table 2.6 shows the growth of Nepalis population in Assam from 1901 to 1951 and their percentage to Assam's total population. Looking from the point of view of marginal farmers we may consider this population as economic working force responsible to the agricultural economic development of Assam.

Table 2.6: The growth of Nepali population in Assam

Year	Population	Percentage
1901	21,347	0.35
1911	47,654	0.67
1921	70,344	0.94
1931	88,306	1.02
1951	1,01,338	1.26

Source: Census of India Reports.

* Report on the Land Revenue Administration of Assam, Valley Division, 1939-40.

Impact of Tea Cultivation on Agriculture

The discovery of wild grown tea plant in Upper Assam by Mr. R.Bruce in 1823 marked the beginning of tea industry in Assam. After successful experiment the British started cultivation of tea from the year 1839 on regular basis. With the beginning of tea cultivation, the economic activities of the province got diversified as it gave impetus to many other sources of economy. Agriculture came to the forefront for providing food for the burgeoning labour population required for tea cultivation. The first Joint Stock Company named Assam Tea Company was established in August, 1845. Gradually, the number of tea gardens grew up and the demand for land increased. The Government passed "Waste Land Rules" on 6 March, 1838 in order to settle large areas of land to Tea Gardens. According to this rule lands were settled to Tea Companies on 45 years lease on condition that one-fourth of the area must be utilized within five years, failing which the land will revert back to the Government. The Land Settlement Rule of 1861 under Fee Simple Grants was more simplified one and the rates of land were minimal as fixed within Rs. 2, Annas 8 and Rs. 5 per acre according to quality of land. As a result of Government encouragement to tea cultivation there was a tremendous growth of tea industry. The area of land under tea cultivation rapidly increased. Table 2.7 shows the area brought under tea gardens up to the year 1915-16.

Table 2.7: Area of land under Tea, in 1895-96 and 1915-16

Districts	**Area under tea cultivation in acres**	
	1895-96	**1915-16**
Goalpara	552	1,247
Kamrup	24,122	23,372
Darrang	1,13,895	1,67,134

(*Contd.*)

Districts	Area under tea cultivation in acres	
	1895-96	1915-16
Nowgong	56,036	47,050
Sibsagar	2,42,432	2,84,128
Lakhimpur	1,87,589	2,45,367
Total	**6,24,626**	**7,65,298**

Source: Assam Land Revenue Manual, 7th edn. 1965, xxxvi-xxxvii.

Simultaneously with the increase in the number of tea gardens, the import of tea labour into Assam also increased from estimated eight lakhs in 1826 to eleven lakhs in 1853 and then to nearly 15 lakhs by 1872.[14] During 1911-1921, according to the Immigrant Labour Report, 7,69,000 tea labours entered Assam (*Census of India*,1951, Vol. 3, Assam, Part I: 45). In 1921 alone 8,12,000 labourers came to Assam. Again during the decade 1921-1931 Assam received 6,95,000 plantation labours. According to E. Gait, the population of tea garden labour including their children in 1921 was 1.3 million or one-sixth of the then Assam's total population. Table 2.8 gives the total tea labour population in Assam from 1911 to 1931.

Table 2.8: Migration of Tea garden workers in Assam

Birth places	1911	1921	1931
Bihar/Orissa	3,99,000	5,71,000	4,72,000

Cattle Rearing Occupation

Cattle rearing and dairy farming is another major occupation of the Gorkhas in Assam. The vast expanse of pastoral lands lying along the river Brahmaputra and the green hills and valleys in Assam attracted the enterprising Gorkhas as early as the middle of the nineteenth century. They came in large number and set up cattle farms (*Goths*) and made it a monopoly occupation. For, no other community was interested in this occupation, even drinking of milk was alien to many people especially the tribals in the hills. The British Government too encouraged the Gorkha herdsmen by constituting Professional Grazing Reserves (PGRs) and Village Grazing Reserves (VGRs) or Village Grazing Grounds (VGGs) at various places around the Brahmaputra banks, *chars* and river derelicts. The profession of cattle rearing in Assam flourished very soon and there was a mushroom growth of cattle farms (*Khuties*) and rapid increase in the cattle population. The Forest Department collected cattle tax at the initial rates of 8 Annas per buffalo and 4 Annas per cow per year (1888) and it became a good source of income for the Government.

Table 2.9 shows an outstanding success achieved by the Nepali graziers of the Brahmaputra valley. The number of buffaloes was increased from 15,640 to 86,327 heads within a span of twenty-five years from 1895 to 1920.

Table 2.9: Number of buffaloes from 1895 to 1920

Year	Number of buffaloes
1895	15,640
1900	18,732
1905	28,346
1910	40,000
1915	42,000
1920	86,325

Corresponding to the increase in the number of cattle, the revenue from this source also increased, making it almost double between 1916-17 and 1920-21 as can be seen from Table 2.10.

Table 2.10: Collection of revenue from grazing tax from 1916-17 to 1920-21

Year	1916-17	1917-18	1919-20	1920-21
Revenue	Rs.1,83,000	Rs. 3,42,000	Rs. 2,77,000	Rs. 3,41,000

Source: A. Guha, *Planters Raj to Swaraj*, 1982, pp. 91-94.

Controversy on Grazing Tax

The Government kept on raising the rates of grazing tax from time to time. In 1986, the tax was 4 Annas per buffalo which was raised to 8 Annas in 1888; then again in 1907 grazing tax per buffalo was increased to Re. 1 which went up to Rs. 2 per buffalo and 6 Annas for other horned cattle in 1915. This rate was finally raised to Rs. 3 for each buffalo and 6 Annas for other horned cattle. There was often resentments from the graziers for raising cattle tax to such an height when the cattle use to graze on the "unclassed state forest" which was just a natural grown vegetation. Ultimately, the matter caught the notice of the legislators and it came up for discussion in the Legislative Council to find out the justification, if any, to levy grazing tax. The honourable member of the Legislative Council of Assam, Mr. Rohini Kanta Hati Baruah, moving a resolution for abolition of the grazing tax said:

> "Sir, this is not a new resolution before this House. I believe no other resolution than this has come so often before this Council. There has not been a single session without a discussion on this subject. Public opinion on this subject has grown ever since and is now decided. People are vehemently opposed to such a tax. If we look at the pages of the Council proceedings even of the pre-Reform days we find

> that this tax has been as unpopular than as ever and public opinion on the subject is very much articulate on this."[15]

It is seen that the grazing tax was imposed under the Assam Forest Regulation where it was provided that any person grazing his cattle on the "Unclassed State Forest" has to pay grazing tax. This means that under the definition of "Unclassed State Forest" falls any waste land in a village that might be classified as unclassified forest. The term wasteland appears to denote those tracts of land which were uncultivated, unsettled and therefore, accruing no revenue to the Government. Wasteland, thus include the forest and highland having extensive high reed and grass, and grassland.[16] The procedure of collection of tax and the punishment meted out in case of default were very severe. If any grazier fails to pay tax in time, he has to pay a fine of Re. 1 in case of Buffalo. In case of any grazier transferred his herd of cattle from one place to another without informing the authorities, then he was liable to be fined or even imprisoned.[17] Apart from above, the tax was levied on all the cattle by head count, irrespective of big or small without any concern about their productivity. Most of the members of the Legislative Council opined that this was unscientific and therefore, Government should impose tax only on the cattle producing milk. Another point raised by the Legislators was that grazing tax should be levied only on the foreigner (Nepali) professional graziers and the indigenous non-professional graziers should be exempted. There was allegations of tax being imposed on the ordinary cultivators as well. On this, the Government Finance Member, A.W.Botham replied that there was not a single Assamese cultivator taxed in the Lakhimpur district for grazing his cattle.[18] Finally, the resolution sought to be passed by the members of the Legislative Council on 24 February, 1926 for abolition of the grazing tax was defeated by a margin of two votes.[19] This was, undoubtedly a very important resolution and had it been passed in the Legislative Council of Assam, the Nepali graziers would have been greatly benefited. The members of the Council who voted for and against of the motion were as follows. (Ayes 12 and Noes 14)

For the Resolution: Shri Brajendra Narayan Choudhury, Gopendralal Das Choudhury, Kshirod Chandra Dev, Bepin Chandra Ghose, Mahadev Sarma, Padmanabh Sarma, Rohini Kanta Hati Baruah, Sarbeswar Baruah, Maulavi Diwan, Abdul Rahim Choudhury, Maulavi Abdul Hanan Choudhury, Maulavi Sayid Abdul Mannan, Maulavi Faiznur Ali,

Against the Resolution: Khan Bahadur Kutubuddin Ahmed, A.W. Botham, Finance Member, Rai Bahadur Pramod Chandra Dutta, Maulavi Sayid Muhammad Saadulla, Chief Minister, G.E. Soames, B.A.Blenkinsop, A.H.W. Bentinck, G.T. Lloyd, J.R. Cunningham, J.C. Evans, Krishna Sundar Dam, Maulavi Rashid Ali Laskar, Lt. Col. H.C. Garbett, and H.B. Buchanan.

The Assam Association took up the lead in the protest against the Government increasing the grazing fees and tightening of collection machinery during the year 1914-1920. It expressed its concern over the issue in its meeting held at Gauhati on 9th October, 1914 and in its Annual Session at Gauhati in 1916 and also at Sibsagar in 1917. In these meetings resolutions were taken up strongly protesting against the oppressive grazing tax imposed by the Government and demanding a total abolition of such tax. Later in April, 1918 Phani Dhar Chaliha, member of the Council had put up a resolution in the Legislative Council for total abolition of grazing tax. However, the fate of the resolution was pre-destined; it was lost as usual, for lack of majority support. The Assam Legislative Council was so formed that the European members who supported the Government were always greater in number. All the thirteen numbers of Government nominated members used to be the Europeans with the exception of one or two; all the three elected planter members were also Europeans, and the Chief Commissioner being the President, out of the total strength of twenty-five member the majority were always on the side of the Government. Thus, a close examination of the composition of the Legislative Council shows that the European members, together with one or two Indian official members, had always an assured majority in the house. The Government of Assam kept on increasing the cattle tax despite frequent discussion and resentment expressed by the members of the Legislative Council. Table 2.11 shows the revenue collected by the Government out of cattle tax as well as the increase of cattle population in Assam during the period from 1910 to 1925.

Table 2.11: Number of cattle population and cattle tax collected during 1910 to 1925 in Assam.

Particulars	1910-11	1915-16	1920-21	1025-26
No. of cattle assessed	12,993	44,199	1,35,690	1,82,605
No. of Graziers	90	184	6,626	9,165
Revenue collected	Rs. 12,525	Rs. 64,007	Rs. 3,01,077	Rs. 3,61,947

Source: ALCP-1928, Vol. I, Part IV, pp. 81-89.

Cattle Rearing in the Hills

The civilian Nepalis and Gorkha ex-servicemen who settled down in the hill districts of Assam carried out cattle rearing as their profession as early as 1860s. "There is a hill, send up a Gorkha" was the avowed principle followed by the British for rehabilitation of the retired Gorkha soldiers.[20] Cattle rearing, as an occupation, was initiated for the first time by the Gorkhas in the hill areas of Assam. The hill people neither used bullock for ploughing the field nor took milk or milk products as their food. Shifting cultivation was their method of agriculture operation where no animal power was necessary, and meat was their traditional diet instead of milk. The Mughal historian, Muhammad Kazim, in this book wrote that the people of Assam never used *ghee* in their food.[21] Even in the Brahmaputra valley, the Assamese people never carried out cattle rearing as primary occupation as there was no demand for milk and milk products. The price of milk in Darrang district was two Annas per seer and that of *ghee* was fourteen Annas for a seer.

In the hill districts of Assam, the Nepalis found the cold climate and the lush green hills and valleys identical with their own country Nepal and also congenial climate for rearing live-stock. Evidences are galore about keeping of large *Bathans* (Goths) by Nepalis in Khasi and Jaintia Hills, Manipur, Garo Hills, NEFA (now Arunachal Pradesh), North Cachar Hills and many other hill areas of the North East.

We have documentary evidence that in Khasi Hills the Gorkha soldiers were first brought in 1829 to quell down U Tirot Singh, the Syiem of Nongkhlaw who resisted opening of a road to Sylhet through Khasi hills. In 1832 Cherrapunjee was made the Headquarters of the 44th Sylhet Light Infantry which comprised a sizeable number of Gorkhas. In 1864 this infantry was shifted to Shillong and converted into 8th Gorkha Rifles. Since that time the retired Gorkha soldiers settled permanently in Shillong many of whom took up the profession of cattle rearing and producing milk, butter and *ghee* for the Shillong inhabitants. The cattle rearing activities among the Nepalis started gathering momentum after Shillong became a Regimental Centre (Gorkha home) in 1869 and many Nepalis came to settle down around the Shillong Regimental Centre.

Initially *Bathans* (Goths) were set up in the outskirts of Shillong like Mawlai, Nongthymmai, Laitumkhrah which in those day, were covered with forests. Later on they shifted to the far-flung hill areas of Mairang, Nongstoin, Maheshkhola, Bhoirymbong etc. with the consent of the Syiem/Sirdars and Lyngdohs. The grazing areas, however, not being especially reserved for cattle grazing purpose and there being *jhum* fields of the local Khasi people all around, many times cattle destroyed the crops. For this damage and loss of crops, the graziers had to compensate by paying heavy fines imposed by the village Durbar. Apart from this, the graziers had to pay heavy grazing tax per head of the cows and buffalo. More often than not, cattle entering the *jhum* fields were caught and killed by the local Khasis.

Despite all these adverse conditions, the Nepalis carried on cattle rearing in Khasi Hills for many years in cordial socio-cultural relations with the local inhabitants. Living together side by side for a long time they mixed up their culture and language. The Nepalis spoke the Khasi language fluently and the Nepali womenfolk wore *jain kyrshah* (thin printed cotton clothe knotted at shoulder and covering the body up to foot) like Khasi women. They exchanged each others' culture and language. The Nepalis introduced the use of milk (drinking of milk with tea) among the Khasis for the first time, which they never did before. In Gazetteer of Bengal and North-East India, B.C. Allen said—"The Khasis do not milk their cows, and in many places do not use the plough, cattle being chiefly kept for the sake of the manure they yield and for food."[22] They also initiated a number of Nepali words into Khasi vocabulary which have become a part of the Khasi language today. The Himalayan coral beads (golden-red) called "Puwaḷa" in Nepali, and worn by

Nepali women as necklace combined with gold, has become a part of Khasi traditional ornament of high value and regard. The Khasis call it "Paila" (derived from Nepali "Puwala") and wear it as necklace elaborately designed with gold as the Nepalis do. The place names like Mahadewkhola Dhankheti, Naspatighari, Nayabangla, Lalchanbasti etc. are all Nepali terms.

The system of open field cattle rearing in the Khasi and Jaintia Hills, in course of time, proved unprofitable. The Nepalis started to switch over to confined cattle farming system with high yielding varieties of cows *viz.*, Jersey, Holstein Friesian, Hariyana etc. By the years 1940s, the progress of dairy farming in Shillong reached its nadir and some of the cattle firms became well known by the names like—Harihar Dairy, Hill Green Dairy and Assam Dairy. These dairies supplied milk and milk products, like butter, cream, *ghee* etc. to the whole Shillong town including all hotels, restaurants and hospitals. Unfortunately, the Nepalis of Khasi Hills received the greatest shock and setback in 1987 due to the ethnic violence targeted against them by the Khasi Students Union (KSU). At least ten Nepalis lost their lives, innumerable of them were injured, a dozen of school buildings were set fire on, and nearly twenty thousand Nepalis left for Nepal selling out their high yielding variety costly cows at thrown away prices. Today, sad to say, almost all the dairy farms of Nepalis have become defunct due to the turn of events extremely adverse to the Nepalis in Khasi and Jaintia Hills.

In Manipur, Nepalis are reported to have started grazing profession in Mantripokhari from 1815, in Pangai in 1880, Toribari in 1910, Kalapahad in 1934 and in Laimakhong in 1961.[23] The Gorkhas were given homestead land and grazing grounds in the northern part of the state and issued *Patta* as landownership documents to each Gorkha settlers. In 1905, B.C. Allen has written in the *District Gazetteers of Nagaland and Manipur* as follows:

> "Considerable herds of buffaloes are kept by Nepalese settlers at the northern end of the valley and a special reserve has been set apart for these herdsmen in the Khoga valley south of Moirang to avoid the endless disputes which have been caused by the animals damaging crops, when graziers were allowed to settle in the neighbourhood of villages. Grazing tax were levied at the rate of 8 Annas for each buffalo and 4 Annas for each small herd of horned cattle."[24]

In Manipur cattle rearing was first started by the retired Gorkha soldiers who were followed by others gradually. The cattle rearing commenced sporadically in the province since 1824 but the fact that the activity took off from 1930s is supported by various documents. For instance, the K.K. Reserve (Kangpokpi-Kanglatombi Reserve) also known as Gorkha Grazing Ground was granted by Government in 1919. This reserve was created especially for the purpose of cattle rearing and it was fifteen miles in length and ten miles in breadth and located between Sekmai and Kangpokpi.[25] The graziers had to pay two types of taxes annually; Rs. 4 per animal as grazing tax and Re. 1 per person as foreigner tax. With the passage of time when the Nepalis population increased, additional area of lands was extended to include Maram, Siddim Pukhri, Irang Part I and Part II. Although initially the Meitei tribe were averse to use milk as their food, in course of time they started to take milk and milk products. As the population of Manipur increased, the demand for milk also rose which motivated Nepali graziers to set up more Goths. In 1971, a Dairy Co-operative Society with twenty-five grazier members came to be started in Imphal town to meet the growing demand. However, the Co-operative Society had to be closed down due to foreigners agitation of 1980s.

The Nepalis have contributed to the growth and development of Manipur in various ways, even by sacrificing their lives. It may be remembered that Subedar Niranjan Chhetri was a close associate of Jubraj Tikendrajit Singh who fought against the British to save his country. Subedar Niranjan Chhetri was arrested and hanged to death by the British in 1891 for the charge of waging a war against the Government.

In the United Mikir and North Cachar Hills, the Nepali cattle rearers penetrated deep into the interior villages and established their cattle Bathans.[26] They are also said to have introduced cultivation of maize (*Makai*) among the local people which became popular staple food of the hills. Large number of Nepali graziers were found in the Changlang district of Arunachal Pradesh who were reported to have settled there since 1826. It was Captain Neufville who settled Gorkhas in Singpho dominated areas of Miao, Diyon etc., the present Changlang district in 1826. Captain Hannay, Major White and Captain Vetch too helped Gorkha settlement subsequently after 1841.[27]

Eviction of Goths (*Khutis*)

In the beginning the Nepali graziers had put up their Bathans (*Khutis*) in the Kajiranga forest by paying regular taxes to the Forest Department. They continued this process for many years. Gradually, as the Bathans increased and number of cattle grew up phenomenally they constructed dwelling houses and brought their families too, to live with them.

In 1903-1904, the Government decided to convert Kajiranga into a Reserved Forest. On 3 January, 1908, the Kajiranga Reserved Forest was formally established with an area of 57,273[28] acre where Nepali graziers were keeping their cattle. The reserve area was further increased by Government in 1913. Unfortunately, the innocent Nepali graziers were completely unaware of the fact of conversion into reserve forest and they continued to graze their cattle on payment of grazing tax. The Government of India was well aware of the existence of a large number of Nepali Khutis within the declared reserved area and thus, it allowed them to be there undisturbed and continued to collect grazing tax. The matter remained in that stage for a long period of fifteen years while the Nepali graziers continued to pay grazing tax to the Forest Department regularly. In 1920, the matter came up for consideration of the Government once again on the question whether the presence of Nepali Khutis within the Game Sanctuary could cast any harmful effect upon the natural ambience of the existing flora and fauna. After taking into consideration about the presence of large number of Nepali graziers cattle farm, the Chief Commissioner considered that the presence of herds of tamed buffaloes in the locality can, sooner or later, transmit cattle disease to the wild animals in the game reserve and the valuable natural fauna of the province might be destroyed and would ultimately defeat the whole purpose of having Reserved Forest. Hence, in 1920, the Government ordered to evict all the Nepali Khutis forthwith within 24 hours. No prior information or order to shift the Khutis was passed on to the Nepali graziers. It was a sure case of miscarriage of natural justice for not allowing even seven days time to the Nepali graziers when the Government kept the matter dragging for long fifteen years. This reflects sharply on the colonial government's arrogance and lack of sympathy towards the law abiding graziers.

On fateful day, in 1920, a full battery of Forest officials accompanied by armed police arrived at the scene and set fire on the cattle sheds and dwelling houses of the Nepali graziers numbering hundred and one families. No prior notice was served nor a reasonable time was allowed to them to salvage/remove their house-hold goods. No requests, prayers or cries were heard.

Within minutes, their houses, cattle sheds including house-hold goods, wearing apparels and even a number of cows and buffalo calves kept confined inside the cattle sheds were burnt into ashes. Such an unjust and inhuman act of the British Government mortally hurt the sentiments of the loyal and peaceful Nepali graziers. Shri Chhabilal Upadhyaya was one of the victims who was personally present at the place of occurrence and tried his level best to resist the forceful eviction. The Nepalis became totally disillusioned and grievously pained resulting in turning rebellious against the colonial rule. What the law abiding Nepalis hurt the most is not the decision of the Government to shift their Khuties from Kajiranga Reserve Forest, but the way the eviction operation was conducted by the Forest Department. After having dragged its feet for long fifteen years over the matter, the department now had no patience for even a couple of days to allow the graziers to shift by themselves. They collectively looked for a course of action which would protect them and provide them with collective safety, security and freedom from future oppression. Finally, they found the right opportunity; the Assamese political leaders who were acting against the British rule invited the Nepalis of Assam under the leadership of Babu Chhabilal Upadhyaya to fight together for their common cause. The Nepalis thus decided to come under the banner of Assam's political organization under the collective leadership of Babu Chhabilal Upadhyaya, Chandranath Sarme, Ramlal Upadhyaya, Bigiram Saikia, Hari Prasad Upadhyaya and others.

A historic meeting of the "Assam Association" was held at Jorhat, Assam on the 17 April, 1921 to decide on the issue of its merger with Assam Provincial Congress and on the future course of action in respect of specific problems faced by the people of Assam. The meeting was presided over by Babu Chhabilal Upadhyaya which marked the turning point of the political history of Assam and also the fate of the Nepalis living in Assam. The meeting adopted a historic decision to merge the Assam Association with the Assam Provincial Congress Party affiliated to the Indian National Congress and to join in the non-cooperation movement of Mahatma Gandhi. With this, the Assam Association which was formed about two decades ago in 1903 by Manik Chandra Baruah came to its end. The meeting also decided to bring the Gorkhas of Assam under the fold of the Congress and to take up the issue of Kajiranga eviction of graziers with the Government of Assam. Thus, the eviction of the Nepali graziers in 1920 may be considered as an event-setter towards the joining in the freedom movement of India by the Nepalis of Assam. They joined the National Congress Party under the leadership of Babu Chhabilal Upadhyaya and Assamase leaders like Tarunram Phukan, Nabin Chandra Bordoloi, Dr. Hem Chandra Baruah, Amiya Kumar Das, Kuladhar Chaliha, Gopinath Bordoloi etc. and actively participated in the *Swadeshi Andolan* of Mahatma Gandhi.

After the Nepali herdsmen were evicted from the Kajiranga forest, the Government provided alternative grazing areas by declaring new PGRs and VGRs along the Brahmaputra river banks, islands and derelict waste lands for grazing their cattle. This act of the Government was motivated by its own interest for the benefit for revenue income rather than for helping the Nepali graziers. As the time passed, new developments started taking place. The Government of Assam, under the ministry of Shaadulla as the Chief Minister, began to give settlement of waste lands to Muslim immigrants in the name of so-called "Grow More Food". The unclassed forest lands of Assam having been exhausted the Mymensingias even encroached upon the PGR lands reserved for grazing cattle. Under the emerging adverse situation faced by the Nepali graziers Babu Chhabilal Upadhyaya and a few other Nepali leaders felt the necessity of forming an organization of the graziers for the safeguard of their common interest. Accordingly in 1933, they formed an association named "Tezpur Graziers' Association" under the chairmanship of Babu Chhabilal Upadhyaya with the following objectives.

(1) Protection and Preservation of Grazing Lands in Assam.
(2) To stop cultivation in professional grazing reserves.
(3) To prevent encroachment of Burachhapari PGR by the Muslim immigrants.
(4) To protect and preserve Assam forest for survival of Nepali graziers.
(5) To join in the national movement for the freedom of India.
(6) To promote social integration between Assamese and Nepali communities.

Through this association, the Nepali graziers could raise their concerted voice against the Government action of large scale settlement of waste lands given to the East Bengal immigrants and also against the encroachment on the grazing reserves. Many Assamese leaders extended their co-operation in this work. The Association even took up fights against the Mymensing encroachers under the leadership of Prasad Singh Subba.

The Budachapori PGR constituted in 1881 was one of the biggest PGR situated at Brahmaputra river-island to the south of Tezpur town. The Nepali graziers of Burachhapori PGR managed their dairy business in organized way by forming an association named the Tezpur Graziers' Association for supply of milk and milk products to Tezpur town. The Tezpur Graziers'Association was formed in 1933 in a meeting held at Singri under the chairmanship of Chhabilal Upadhyaya as its founder President. The objectives of the Association were—

(1) protection and preservation of grazing lands in Assam,
(2) to stop cultivation in professional grazing reserves,
(3) prevention of encroachment of Burachhapari by immigrants,
(4) protection of forest as environment,
(5) to involve domiciled Nepalis of Assam in the freedom movement of India,
(6) promote social harmony and integration between Assamese and Nepali communities.

The Graziers' Association initially started grazing cattle in the Burachhapori professional grazing reserve and gradually occupied other reserves around it like—Kampani Tapu, Lame Tapu, Bhaunne Tapu, Ramai Tapu, Lamsalay Tapu, Lahareni Tapu, Khalai Tapu, Solebali Tapu, Betkati, Aam Tapu, Baralimara, Charghare, Karne, Naste, etc. Like Tapu, "Chhapadi" is another Nepali name for "Char" or river derelict island. Nepali graziers established a number of villages in these "Chhapadis" along the banks of the river Brahmaputra from Biswanath Ghat to Buroi river for their habitation and cultivation. Some of these habitations are—Asare Chhapadi, Surbire Chhapadi, Musaldari Chhapadi, Lasune Chhapadi etc. The names of the villages and the khuties mentioned above are typically Nepali language. Although majority of these villages were inhabited by Nepali Brahmin and Chhetris, some of them had mixed population of Assamese and Nepali who lived together. Both the communities mixed up their cultures and languages and lived in harmony and good relations. The Assamese people cordially co-operated with Nepalis in celebration of Durga Puzas, Tehar, Teez etc. while the Nepalis actively participated in Assamese festivals like Bihu, Rash Lila, Sankardev Tithi etc. with all gaiety and fervour. Nepali Freedom Fighters like Babu Chhabilal Upadhyaya, Bishnulal Upadhyaya, Ramlal Upadhyaya, Hari Prasad Upadhyaya, Prasad Singh Subba etc. had their Goths (*Khutis*) in these PGRs. During his youth Babu Chhabilal Upadhyaya was an adventurous man and a good swimmer too. He used to demonstrate his courage and acumen by catching floating timber logs during high flood in the river Brahmaputra. Many of the Nepali elites like Dharmananda Upadhyaya, Narad Chandra Upadhyaya, Krishna Prasad Upadhyaya, Tikaram Sarma etc. had passed their early boyhood days in these Khuties. Tikaram Sarma once related to me about a horrific incident of instant killing of his boy servant by an wild buffalo at his Khuti. The wild buffaloes often used to come to the Khuti with their domestic female buffaloes during their heat period. One day a huge male wild buffalo came to his Khuti with one of his domestic female buffalo, and as soon as the servant boy unknowingly approached the female buffalo, the wild buffalo attacked him with his long horn piercing through his belly for which the boy died instantly. It was, thus, always dangerous on the part of the Khuti dwellers to be attacked by wild animals like tigers, elephants and buffaloes. Many of the herdsmen used to have their wives and children lived with them in the khuties and they have to be extra careful from these dangers. The khuties were their well-loved home where the children grew up and started their education and training in cattle rearing. They had also the tradition of celebrating Dasain (Devi Puza), Tewhar in the Tapus. Later, in 1822 the celebration of Devipuza was shifted to Gangmouthan (Majgaon) and since that time, the Nepali population of this village grew up in large number.

In 1930, the Chief Secretary of the Government of Assam wrote to the Foreign Secretary to the Government of India that the greater number of the numerous Nepali graziers in Assam are Jaisis and Upadhyaya Brahmins or Chhetris of non-martial class. Some of the Gorkhalis of the fighting class who have served in the Gurkha Regiments in Assam Rifles, settled down in Assam after retirement from their services.[29] In this context it may be stated that the tradition of cattle rearing, as a pastoral occupation of the Nepalese Brahmins/Chhetris has come down as a legacy from "the earliest rulers of Nepal who belonged to the "Gopala (cow-herds) and Mahisapalas (buffalo-herds) dynasties."[30] Cattle, especially cow rearing was considered as a sacred profession by the Hindus in Nepal, and the Government of Nepal accorded a special status to the cow by providing it legal protection. The killing of a cow entails a punishment equal to the killing of a human being. Another reason why Brahmins took up cattle rearing occupation, instead of farming was that, the Brahmins were forbidden by Vedic tradition to hold the plough for cultivation. This is, the logical explanation of the Nepali Brahmins resorting to cattle rearing in Assam.

Nepali Graziers *versus* Muslim Immigrants

Assam had a large Muslim population migrated from the East Bengal. The immigration into Assam began even before the advent of colonial rule. Historically, the immigration of Muslims into the North East India started before the arrival of the Ahoms who ruled Assam for long 600 years. But these Muslims fully merged with Assamese community and become Asamiya in course of time. After the British annexed Assam following the treaty of Yandaboo in 1826, the district of Sylhet was incorporated into Assam in 1874. This opened the flood gate of Muslim immigration into Assam from the Muslim majority province of East Bengal. The migration of East Bengal peasants first took place to the then thinly populated Goalpara district, and then from there to Kamrup, Nowgong and Darrang districts of the Brahmaputra valley. After the Saadulla Ministry was formed in Assam in 1937 especially from the 25 August, 1942 large number of Muslim immigrants from East Bengal were allowed to come and settle down in Assam. They were liberally allotted waste lands for their settlement and livelihood in every nook and corner of Assam wherever space was available not sparing even waterlogged, jungle-infested and riverine belts. "All that they wanted was land. From their riverine base they further pressed themselves forward in all directions in search of more living space in the areas held by the autochthons."[31] Table 2.12 shows decadal growth of Muslim population in Assam during 1921–51.

Table 2.12: Decadal growth of Muslim population in Assam During 1921–1951

Year	Total population	Muslim population	Muslim growth rate
1921	45,93,572	8,68,639	–
1931	55,03,518	12,66,985	45.8%
1941	66,33,683	16,84,350	32.9%
1951	79,70,998	19,80,780	17.6%

Source: Census of India, Reports of relevant years.

When all possible space were exhausted they even began to encroach upon the Professional Grazing Reserves allotted to the Nepali graziers for grazing cattle. The Mymensinghias had noticeably invaded many areas of Brahmaputra valley even during the mid-colonial period which is evidenced by the following remarks by C.S. Mullan, the then Superintendent of Census 1931 who wrote about the invasion of the "immigrant army".

> "...(the Muslims) has almost completed the conquest of Nowgong. The Barpeta Sub-division of Kamrup has also fallen to their attack and Darrang is being invaded. Sibsagar has so far escaped completely, but the few thousand Mymensinghias in North Lakhimpur are an outpost which, may during

> next decade, prove to be a valuable basis for major operations. Wheresoever the carcass, there the vultures be gathered together; where there is wasteland thither flock the Mymensinghias." (Census Report 1931–51)

This statement of C.S. Mullan came in handy for Ambikagiri Ray Choudhury for his campaign against the Muslims while the Assamese intelligentsia started being scared of the fast increasing number of Bengali speaking Muslim peasants who had begun to dominate the local economy. Shri Mahadev Sarma came forward with his resolution in the Assam Legislative Council for taking immediate steps to curb the influx of the Mymensinghiyas from Bengal which, however, did not get full-fledged support from the members. Even many Assamese leaders did not seem to hear the alarm bell sounded by the report of C.S Mullan as they remained blissfully silent.

Mahammad Sayd Saadulla, took charge of the office of the Chief Minister (Prime Minister in those days) of Assam on 1st April, 1937 as the head of Non-Congress coalition ministry. One Abdul Hamid Khan better known as Mawlana Bhasani, took full advantage of bringing Bengali speaking Muslims into Assam under various pretext, with the ultimate plan of fulfilling the secret objective of the All India Muslim League to turn Assam into a Muslim majority province and to merge it with East Bengal. This person named Abdul Hamid Khan came from Pabna district of the then East Bengal and settled in the Char area of Goalpara district called Bhasani char and thereby came to be known as Maulana Bhasani, espoused the cause of the immigrant Muslims and became their leader. Later on, he rose to be the President of Assam Provincial Muslim League and the right hand of Saadulla in carrying out the works for Muslim community. On the plea of "Grow more Food" programme, the

Bengal Legislative Council adopted a resolution on 16 July, 1943 calling upon the Government of India to take immediate steps to remove all existing restrictions imposed by Assam Government on the East Bengal Muslim cultivators from migrating into Assam. Taking this advantage the Saadulla Ministry of Assam adopted a similar resolution of "Grow more Food" on 24 August, 1943 with the following specific objectives:

1. To distribute wasteland in proportion to the needs of the different communities in Nowgong and de-reservation of select Grazing Reserves for that purpose.
2. De-reservation of Professional Grazing Reserves in Kamrup and Darrang if found surplus to actual requirement.
3. Opening up surplus reserves in all submontane areas and in Sibsagar and Lakhimpur for settlement of landless indigenous people.

Source: Assam Tribune, 3 September, 1943 and AIR, July, December,1943, Vol. II, pp. 279-80.

The Grow more Food programme of Saadulla ministry was, widely criticized by press media and political parties ironically calling it as "Grow more Muslim" scheme in the guise of food production. Mawlana Bhasani, however, carried the day. The work of de-reservation and settlement of Muslim immigrants went ahead as intended. Vast areas of Professional grazing Reserves were de-reserved and large number of Nepali Khuties were evicted. There was no one to protest on behalf of the gullible Nepali graziers. The most tragic incident was that, side by side with the Government settlement to the Muslim cultivators, there was large scale illegal encroachment on the grazing reserves by the Muslim immigrants with apparent connivance of the Government machinery.

In September,1943 Government appointed one IAS officer, S.P. Desai to enquire and report whether there existed any more Professional Grazing Reserve in surplus to requirement that could be de-reserved for giving settlement to the East Bengal Muslim immigrants. Mr. Desai held spot enquiry and reported to the Government that forcible occupation of grazing lands by immigrants had already taken place to a large scale, even in predominantly Assamese and tribal areas. Hence, he reported that there was no surplus Professional Grazing Reserve available for new settlement. (*Assam Tribune*, Editorial, dated 27 October,1944). But ignoring this report of a senior IAS officer, the Saadulla and Muslim League coalition Government threw open many Professional Grazing Reserve, for settlement of Muslim immigrants. A delegation of the affected Nepali graziers waited upon the Chief Minister and the Governor of Assam under the leadership of Chhabilal Upadhyaya for rehabilitation of the evicted families but no action whatsoever was taken. The Government put a deaf year even to the hew and cry raised by the Assamese indigenous people under the banner of Assam Jatiya Mahasabha against the settlement of Bengali Muslim immigrants in Assam.

In February, 1946, Gopinath Bordoloi's Congress ministry came to power. The first ever action taken by his Government was to start eviction of Muslim immigrants who were encroaching the Professional Grazing reserves. Maulana Bhasani came forward to protest against the eviction of Muslims as the President of the Provincial Muslim League Action Committee. The immigrants resisted eviction and fought pitched battles with the police who fired killing about fifteen people. Maulana Bhasani sought the help of Jinna, the President of the All India Muslim League who rushed to Gauhati on 7th April, 1946 and held public meeting condemning Bordoloi Government. The Government put a deaf ear and decided to go ahead with eviction. Bhasani fired next salvo by beginning a fast unto death and demanding resettlement of the evicted Muslims into their lands while the Government answered it with promulgation of the Assam Maintenance of Public Order Act and put a stop to all agitations.

On several occasions, the Muslim immigrants attacked Nepali khuties and threatened to kill them in order to drive them away from the grazing reserve with the sole intention of occupying the reserve. On 27 November, 1946, the *Statesman* daily newspaper published a sensational news stating that about 300 Muslim immigrants armed with *lathis* and other weapons attacked Nepali professional graziers on 9th November at a place in Guwahati Sub-division. Seven men were injured, five buffaloes were killed and several others were injured. The attackers took away properties of the graziers and also a number of their buffaloes. Four immigrants were arrested. Attempts were also made recently at a number of villages in Mangaldoi Sub-division to terrorise the permanent inhabitants. To prevent the condition from getting worse the authorities had to promulgate orders under Sec. 144 Cr. PC prohibiting assembly of more than four persons and carrying of weapons. Government has also been empowered to take steps to control public meetings and processions and maintain essential services. A member of the Assam Cabinet said—"We are tackling every potential source of danger to the peace and tranquility of the province and are determined to erase it when it appears. Unless people who were defying the law of the land were duly dealt with they would commit other acts of lawlessness. ...They were concentrated mostly in Kamrup, Darrang, Nawgong and Sibsagar districts, forcibly occupying grazing reserves, waste lands and also lands owned by indigenous people."[32] During the last twenty years considerable areas of lands had been settled by Government to the immigrants, but the demand for more land could never be met resulting in enchroaching lands set apart as potential grazing reserves where Nepali graziers keep large herds of cattle on payment of grazing tax as high as rupees three per buffalo to the Government.

Eviction of the Muslim immigrants from encroachment of grazing reserves in Kamrup, Darrang and Sibsagar districts was started in May 1947 and more than 3,000 encroachers were evicted. They were given fifteen days notice to vacate the land which they never complied. Rather strong opposition to Governments eviction policy came from the Muslim League. The Secretary of the Assam Provincial Muslim League in a statement said that these helpless people have no other place to go to and if, in spite of this, attempts are made to evict them from the land they have settled in, the result would be disastrous.

Nepalis as Industrial Labours

During the middle of nineteenth century Assam passed through a period of tremendous growth of industries like tea, coal, petroleum and railway expansion for which a large number of labour was required. Coal mining being a labour intensive industry there was a need of large number of workers. The indigenous Assamese people refused to work in coal mines. The Naga labourers were initially engaged but they were scared to go deep into the tunnels. The choice, therefore, fell on the Gorkha labourers who were hard workers and not scared of dying. Large number of Gorkha workers were imported from Jalpaiguri and Duors areas with the help of Gorkha Thikadars.

In 1825, petroleum deposit was discovered in Digboi areas and the first oil well was dug near Jaypore in 1866. Thereafter, the drilling of oil mines progressed so fast that in 1893 several wells were drilled one after another in Digboi, Nagarkatia,

Moran, Rudrasagar, Sonari, Amguri, Geleki etc. To meet the increased demand for labour, a large number of Gorkhas from North Bengal, Sikkim and Bhutan were imported to Assam. This affected adversely on the labour requirement for tea gardens in Darjeeling and Duors areas due to which the Government of West Bengal objected to further export of labour. Finally, the problem of labour shortage was resolved in 1919 after an agreement was reached with the Government of Nepal to allow its subjects to be recruited in the coal and petroleum industries of Assam. After this agreement Assam never faced the problem of manpower.

A large number of Gorkha labours were also engaged in the cutting and sawing of timber logs for producing railway sleepers needed for the extension of railway lines all-over Assam. The most unwelcome task inside the malarious and wild animal infested forest of Assam for felling of trees, cutting into logs, sawing and producing millions of railway sleepers needed for Assam could be done by no other than the Gorkha sawyers (*Arawals*) brought from Nepal. During early nineteenth century when the man-power resource was so scarce the enormity of contribution made by the Gorkhas in the development of Assam's economy could have been realized by the British only.

Cultural Integration with Assamese Society

The Gorkhas living in Assam fitted themselves well with the larger Assamese society. Wherever they settled down, be it hills or plains, they adopted the local language, dresses and culture and shared with their problems and prospects. They forgot their erstwhile country Nepal and lost all socio-political interest in it. They loved their new found land as their mother land. Perhaps, it would not be exaggerated to say that, in the present context, the Gorkhas in India are the only one community who adopts other's culture without a whimper and, at the same time, keep their own too. Professor A.C. Sinha, noted Social scientist, remarked—"The Nepalis have a great capacity to assimilate themselves with the hill communities. They adopt the language of their neighbourhood, contract marital alliances and turn out to be an inseparable part of the local economy."[33]

The Gorkhas are a community with sizeable population in Assam, have their rich and diverse culture and heritage and a language (Nepali) whose literature is sufficiently advanced that has found a place in the 8th Schedule of the constitution of India. They want to live in Assam in complete harmony and brotherhood with the local people and at the same time preserve, protect and develop their own culture and language. They would like to identify themselves as Assamese Gorkhas in exclusion of the Nepalese nationals from Nepal.

The Gorkhas of Assam send their children to Assamese medium schools right from Primary to Matriculation standard. This is one of the redeeming traits of the Gorkhas of Assam. They do not want to send their children to Nepali medium school. It is not because they have no money to construct and maintain Nepali medium schools: they have constructed many Assamese medium schools and colleges and donated generously to such schools. For example, in 1941 Chabilal Upadhyaya established Behali High School in the most backward Behali Mauza which imparts education to children of all communities till today but he never wanted to introduce Nepali medium in that school. Many Nepali Mahajans have generously donated to a number of educational institutions in various parts of Assam, like, Darrang College at Tezpur, Bhim Bahadur Vidyapith (MV School), Buda Chapari M.E. School, Behali MV School, Prajapati Rijal Higher Secondary School, Gamiri, Shingari, Nikasi, Sholong, Lekhapani, Purbanchal High School etc.

Gorkhas in Politics

The politically naïve and simple Gorkhas did no longer remain aloof from the politics. For, centuries ago Greek statesman, Pericles (495-429 BC) said—"Just because you don't take interest in politics, does not mean that politics won't take interest in you". This universal truth materialized among the Gorkhas in 1920 when the British Government perpetrated an act of cruelty on the innocent Gorkha herdsmen by carrying out a mass eviction from Kajiranga Reserve Forest. It was this incident which aroused a strong resentment of the simple Gowalas against the British rule and that marked the beginning of the national awakening among the Gorkhas of Assam. That was the incident which ignited the conscience of the Gorkhas for unity and co-operation to stand against the repressive British administration. They became politically conscious of the fact that their country and people were being misruled and exploited by the British as foreigner. Babu Chhabilal Upadhyaya, the fore-runner of Gorkha politics joined the Congress Party in the same year and actively took part in Mahatma Gandhi's non-co-operation movement. Babu Chhabilal Upadhyaya presided over the historic meeting of the "Assam Association" held at Jorhat, Assam on the 17 April, 1921 which decided to dissolve "Assam Association" and to form Assam Provincial Congress Committee in its place. The meeting marked the birth of Assam Pradesh Congress Committee and thus Babu Chhabilal Upadhyaya became the father of Assam Congress party. Together with this, other elite Gorkhas of Assam like Hari Prasad Upadhyaya, Tikaram Upadhyaya, Dalbir Singh Lohar, Bhakta Bahadur Pradhan, Bishnulal Upadhyaya, Kumud Chandra Sarma, Devi Prasad Upadhyaya, Anna Purna Devi, Tilarupa Devi etc. joined Assam Congress Party under the leadership of Chhabilal Upadhyaya. Thus, the occasion marked the beginning of the political journey of the Gorkhas living in Assam. They co-operated with Assamese leaders like Chandra

Nath Sarma, Omeo Kumar Das, Gahan Chandra Goswami, Vijay Chandra Bhagabati, Bagiram Saikia etc. and launched political campaigns like *Satygraha*, Civil Disobedience Movement and Quit India Movement. Chhabilal Upadhyaya, his brother Hari Prasad Upadhyaya, Bishnulal Upadhyaya and Kumud Chandra Sarma suffered imprisonment for actively participating in the Quit India Movement. During 1942 movement a large number of Gorkhas of Majgaon, Behali, Sootiya, Jamuguri, Dhekiajuli etc. actively took part in the Quit India Movement and many of them courted arrest and imprisonment.

After independence, India's first general election was held in 1952 to elect members of the Parliament of independent India and the members of the state Legislatures. The Gorkhas did not miss the opportunity to elect their own representatives to the Parliament and state Assemblies for the safeguard of their legal and political rights. They decided to contest election and to wrest as many seats as possible in the Assam Assembly for the sake of welfare and development of the backward Gorkhas of Assam. As a matter of fact, participating in the electoral politics was not a new thing for the Gorkhas of Assam, as they had done so even during the pre-independence period. Dalbir Singh Lohar, one of the prominent Gorkha leaders from Dibrugarh was elected as member of the Assam Legislative Assembly during Gopinath Bordoloi Government (1946–1952). He was a veteran Congress leader from Dibrugarh and a lifelong leader of the Assam Mazdoor Sangh. So, the Gorkhas of Assam, contested the general election of 1952 in which Dalbir Singh Lohar won the election from Dibrugarh constituency. Although Gorkha population in Assam was large enough, they could not succeed well in the elections because of the fact that they were living scattered around various districts and became minority in constituency-wise. However, in some constituencies like Gahapur, Margherita, Nowboicha, Borsola and Mawprem in

Meghalaya there were heavy concentration of Nepali population. Ever since 1952 the Gorkhas of Assam have continued to contest every election for both Lok Sabha and Assembly seats and have been successful in winning a number of seats on every occasion. Bishnulal Upadhyaya succeeded in winning Assam Legislative Assembly seat from Gahapur (Behali) constituency for four times in 1957, 1962, 1967 and 1978 with Congress ticket. D.N. Joshi won Meghalaya Legislative Assembly election as many as six times consecutively from 1972 to 1998 from Mawprem (Shillong) constituency with Congress ticket. Similarly, Kul Bahadur Chhetri won four times and became a Minister in Assam cabinet. Padam Bahadur Chouhan was also a three timer (1978, 1983 and 1985) and occupied a berth in the cabinet of Hiteswar Saikia Government. Tanka Bahadur Rai won election from Borsola constituency for three terms and became Minister and Assembly Speaker in Assam. Gorkha leaders won Lok Sabha seats too—Mani Kumar Subba was elected two times with Congress ticket, Swarup Upadhyaya and Ram Prasad Sharma one time each with Congress and BJP tickets respectively.

NOTES

1. Asad Hussain (1970). *British India's Relations with the Kingdom of Nepal,* p. 185.
2. *Ibid.*, p. 7.
3. Appendix J of A.J.M. Mills Report on the Province of Assam (1854) Reprinted 1984, p. 93.
4. Monirul Hussain (1993). *Assam Movement,* Nanak Publications, New Delhi.
5. T.B. Subba (2003). "The Nepalis in North East India: Political Aspirations and Ethnicity". In *The Nepalis in North East India,* A.C. Sinha & T.B. Subba (eds.), p. 57.
6. *Ibid.*, p. 68.
7. A.J.M. Mills (1854). *Report to Government,* xiv.

8. Sajal Nag, "Politics of People". In *Society and Economy in North-East India,* Vol. III, David R. Syiemlieh/Manorama Sharma (eds.), pp. 110-111.
9. A. Guha (1991). *Medieval and Early Colonial Assam,* New Delhi, p. 9.
10. Sajal Nag, "Politics of People", in *Society and Economy in North-East India,* Vol III, David R. Syiemlieh/Manorama Sharma (eds.), pp. 110-111.
11. H.K. Borpujari (ed.). *Political History of Assam,* Vol. V, p. 48.
12. B.C. Allen (2005). *Gazetteer of Bengal and North East India, 1905* (Reprint by Mittal Publiction, New Delhi, p. 102.
13. Monirul Hussain (1993). *Assam Movement,* Nanak Publications, New Delhi.
14. *Op. cit.,* Amalendu Guha, p. 187.
15. *LCD*, Vol. VI, 1926, p. 236.
16. Mills, A.J.M., *Report on the Province of Assam,* p. 56.
17. *LCD*, Vol. VI, 1926, p. 236.
18. *Ibid.*, p. 239.
19. *Ibid.*, p. 250.
20. E. Chandler (1913). *Unvailing Lhasa,* London.
21. "A Description of Assam", Translated by H.Vansittart, in *Asiatic Research Survey*, Vol. II, p. 132.
22. B.C. Allen (1905). *Gazetteers of Bengal and North-East India,* Reprinted by Mittal Publication, New Delhi, 2005, p. 490.
23. M. Gautam (1999). *Manipurma Nepali Janajivan,* Kanglatumbi, Nepali Sahitya Parishad, pp. 16, 37, 40, 59, 61, 64.
24. B.C. Allen (1905). *District Gazetteers of Nagaland and Manipur.*
25. C. Dubey (1970). "Manipuri Gorkhaliharu", *Assam Gorkha Sammelon Bulletin,* Vol. II, pp. 2-3.
26. *Gazetteer of Assam* (1979), United Mikir and Cachar Hills districts.
27. Khemraj Sarma (2013). *Gorkhas in the Wilderness,* Concept Publushing Company Pvt. Ltd., Delhi, p. 84.
28. *Assam Forest Bulletin,* Vol. 1, No. 1, Department of Forest, Government of Assam, July, 1905.
29. India Office Library Records, MSS/EMR, p. 7607/1930, confidential letter No. 892.
30. Rishikesh Shaha (1975). *An Introduction to Nepal,* Ratna Pustak

Bhandar, Kathmandu.

31. *Op. cit.*, A. Guha, p. 206.
32. Prafulla Kumar Mahanta (1986). *The Tussle Between the Citizens and Foreigners in Assam.*
33. A.C. Sinha (1990). "The Indian North East Frontier and Nepali Immigrants". In *Himalayan Environment and Culture,* N.K. Rustomji and Charles Ramble (eds.), New Delhi, p. 236.

3

Development and Integration of Nepalis Culture in Assam

Culture needs to be protected, preserved and developed so that it is not influenced by other cultures existing around it. For this purpose, there is a need of middle class group of people composed of elite and educated youths in the society. But unfortunately there was no such elite group among Nepali society during the early period of their settlement in the North East. The Nepalis, in those days, were totally averse and indifferent towards education, as they were engaged in their economic pursuits. It was only by the third decade of the twentieth century that a semblance of a small group of elite youths cropped up here and there in the Nepali society. Mani Singh Gurung was the first Nepali who graduated in 1915. Bishnulal Upadhyay passed Matriculation in 1938 from Tezpur Government High School and passed B.A from Cotton College, Guwahati in 1941. Other Nepali youths like Gangadhar Upadhyaya, Loknath Joshi, Pritam Bahadur Chhetri, Druva Nath Joshi from Shillong, Tankanath Upadhyaya, Dharmananda Upadhyaya, Kumud Chandra

Sharma, Bhavani Prasad Upadhyaya, Siv Prasad Upadhyaya etc. from Majgaon (Tezpur area) emerged subsequently from schools and colleges. The Gorkha Pathsala of Shillong was the first Nepali school established in 1876. In 1927, the Hatibandha Primary School was upgraded to Middle Vernacular school and thereafter to Middle English School. Hatibandha Girls MV (Middle Vernacular) School was established for girls at Majgaon, however the question of sending their daughters to school posed a great problem before the orthodox Brahmin society. In 1939, Chabilal Upadhyaya established Behali High School in the Nepali concentrated area. Eventually, the Nepalis realized the value of education. The well-to-do Nepalis demonstrated their wisdom by donating large sums of money to schools and colleges. Devi Prasad Pokhrel donated Rs. 40,000 to Behali High school, Brihaspati Upadhyaya donated Rs. 20,000 to Hari Mandir, Prabhuram Karki donated Rs. 5,000 to Darrang College. A number of educational institutions were built-up in various parts of Assam with the financial help and efforts of Nepalis like, Bhim Bahadur Vidyapith (MV School), Buda Chapari M.E.School, Behali MV School, Prajapati Rijal Higher Secondary School, Gamiri, Shingari, Nikasi, Sholong, Lekhapani, Purbanchal High School etc. All these schools were located in Nepali concentrated areas and helped building up Nepali elite society. Apart from the above mentioned schools, the following schools were also among the old educational institutions established in different parts of the North East:

1.	Gorkha Pathsala	Upper Shillong	1824
2.	Boys Middle School	Aizawl	1922
3.	Sarkari Nepali Pathsala	Aizawl	1925
4.	Didboi Nepali Pathsala	Digboi	1926
5.	AOC Nepali LP.School	Digboi	1942
6.	Ujan Bazar Gorkha ME School	Guwahati	1940

7.	Gorkha MV. L.MB School Uzanbazar	Guwahati	1947
8.	Tura Gorkha Pathsala	Tura	1946
9.	AOC Nepali ME School	Digboi	1947
10.	Tura Gorkha N.MV	Tura	1951
11.	Bokapathar Devicharan LMV	Lakhipathar	1954
12.	Badagaon Nepali Vidyalaya Guwahati	Devkota	1959
13.	Purbanchal Nepali Vidyalaya	Digboi	1962
14.	Gorkha Madhyamik Vidyalaya	Garo Hills	1962
15.	Shishu Vidyalaya	Duliajan	1967

(The list is not exhaustive)

These educational institutions established in early period greatly contributed to building up a strong foundation for future development of Nepali language and culture. This also helped reverse the downward trend and deteriorating social, cultural and political conditions of the Nepalis in the North East.

Side by side with the above educational institutions, a number of social and cultural organizations that came up among the Nepalis also contributed to development of Nepali culture. In 1930, Nepali Theatre Party and a Theatre Hall was established at Majgaon (Behali) for cultural activities. In Shillong, Gorkha Association was formed with various branches like—Cultural Wing, Social Service Wing, Games and Sports Wing, Library etc. Nepali Sahitya Parishad and a Gorkha Library was also set up in Shillong. "Gorkha Sevak" the first Nepali magazine edited by Mani Singh Gurung emerged from Shillong in 1935.

In 1944, an organisation named the Assam Provincial Gorkha League, a branch of the All India Gorkha League, Darjeeling was established in Shillong which was responsible in bringing about a new socio-cultural awakening among the Nepalis in the North East. It may be difficult to believe but true, that till 1944 there did not exist any social, political or cultural association among the vast population of Nepalis living in entire North East India. The AIGL had a profound impact on the Nepalis of the North East in respect of their language, tradition and culture. It brought about a new consciousness of Nepali identity among them and aroused a sense of solidarity as the Indian Nepalis. The word "Gorkha" became so popular and endearing to everybody's heart that they started greeting each other by saying—"Jai Gorkha". The utterance of this magic word brought to them a sense of unity and brotherhood. The AIGL succeeded in earning a tremendous popularity of the Nepalis of North East due to able leadership of Dambar Singh Gurung and his associates. Nepali youths started doing social, cultural and literary activities. Institutions like Youth clubs, Associations, Libraries were established at various places across Assam. The Tezpur Gorkha Chhatra Sangha was formed on 13th November,1946. Pragati Club was established at Behali (Gangmouthan) in 1947. Libraries were established at Tezpur, Jamuguri and Puthimari. In Shillong, Gorkha Association was established in 1956 with its two Branches *viz.*, Cultural Wing and Games and Sports Wing. Mahila Samiti was formed in 1964 and All Shillong Nepali Students Union started working in 1967. The Nepalis in Assam developed their culture, language and literature and succeeded in getting their language Nepali recognized under 8th Schedule of the constitution in 1992 after a long and consistent fight.

Integration with Assamese Culture

The situation during modern age is completely different. This is an age of ethnic assertion, consciousness of language and culture, even to the extent of identity chauvinism and jingoism. The people are not only possessive of their ethnic identity but also zealously concerned for it. They are proud of their language, culture and past heritage. People went to the extent of resorting to violence in order to preserve, protect and develop their own culture, language and religion as it is happening in the North East India. They are totally bereft of the idea of co-existence, secularism and the spiritual ethics of "live and let live".

The second wave of Nepalis that came to Assam during British period were different from the previous group. They came to Assam, nearly two hundred years ago as soldiers of the Indian army. The Gorkhas of Cuttack Legion (later changed the name to Sylhet Light Infantry) set their feet on the soil of Assam in 1817 during the wake of Burmese invasion of Assam. The Gorkhas were instrumental in driving away the Burmese and saving the Assamese people from their barbaric oppression. The Gorkhas came to Assam as recruits in the Indian army and subsequently as civilian immigrants and settled down permanently in Assam. They are multi-cultural and multi-lingual like Assamese people. They have their religion similar (or almost similar) to the Assamese people, their language Nepali born out of the same root (Sanskrit) and their customs and traditions not very different from the people of Assam. Historically speaking, a large section of them, those belonging to Tibeto-Burman linguistic group had their origin in Assam. They were the descendants of Kirata race and their king Ghataka ruled over Kamrupa with his capital at Pragjyotisa[1], who was slain by Naraka. Subsequently, the Kiratas were pushed towards Nepal, Bhutan and the sub-Himalayan regions by the Aryans as they marched into the North Eastern India. Thus, the Nepali's migration into the North East was like their home coming.

The situation during modern time is completely different. The peoples are proud of their language, culture and past heritage. And yet the Nepalis were largely secular minded. The Nepalis living in the North East India are yet the most liberal cosmopolitan minded, accommodating and open to other's culture and language. Wherever they settled down, be it hills or plains, they adjusted themselves with the lifestyle of local tribe or community, adopted their language, dresses and culture and shared with their problems and prospects. Perhaps, it would not be exaggerated to say that, in the present context, the Nepalis in India are the only one community who adopt other's culture without a whimper and, at the same time, keep their own too in tact. They are a community with sizeable population in Assam (5,64,790, Census 2001), have a rich and diverse culture and heritage and a developed language (Nepali) whose literature is sufficiently advanced and has found a place in the 8th Schedule of the Constitution of India. The Nepalis wanted to live in Assam in complete harmony and brotherhood with the local people and at the same time preserve, protect and develop their own culture and language. They would like to identify themselves as Indian Nepalis or Gorkhas in exclusion of the Nepalese nationals from Nepal.

In Assam, the Nepalis fitted themselves well with the larger Assamese society consisting of Assamese, Boros, Rabhas, Kacharis, Garos, Koches etc. most of whom are their consanguinities (Kiratas). They have been here for the last two hundred years. They have lost all socio-political contact with Nepal—their erstwhile country. Vast majority of them have never been to Nepal. They have loved their new found land Assam as their mother land, its surroundings, hills and valleys and the people who live here. They have adapted themselves well with the local people and their language and culture. They have also shared their own culture and language to the people of this land, mostly the tribals of the hill states. In Khasi Hills, they lived for many years in cordial relations with the local inhabitants. Living together side by side for a long time they have mixed up their culture and language. The Nepalis spoke the Khasi language fluently and the Nepali womenfolk wore *jain kyrshah* (thin printed cotton clothe knotted at shoulder and covering the body up to foot) like Khasi women. They exchanged each others' culture and language. A large segment of Nepali population became converted to Christianity. The place names like Mahadewkhola Dhankheti, Naspatighari, Nayabangla, Lalchanbasti etc. are all Nepali terms.

The people of the North East too found them to be simple, similar looking with themselves and *entente cordiale*. Hence they welcomed the Nepalis with their open heart. "They were largely well-accepted and well-treated in larger Assamese society"—was the comment of Manirul Hussain.[2] So they lived together, exchanged their cultures and traditions and at times, mixed their blood in legitimate matrimony, unlike many other communities who have come from outside and lived here for generations. Let me quote here, for example, from some writers about those outsiders living in Assam. Amalendu Guha writes:

> "In course of time the Nepalis became acultured with Assamese in respect of language, culture, tradition, but the Muslim immigrants remained as before even to this day. They even did not mix up with the Assamese Muslims who speak Assamese, follow Assamese culture, except profess Islam. Though they had common religion, the two communities are wide apart in culture, psychological make up and socio-economic condition. Unlike the immigrant Muslims, their Assamese counterparts neither practised "Purda" nor did they have professional zeal for Urdu as status symbol."[3]

Journalist, Shekhar Gupta writes about the Bengalis in Assam in his book entitled—"A Valley Divided":

> "There is no denying the fact that over the years Bengali cultural and linguistic arrogance has also

> contributed to this syndrome. The Bengali Hindu has by and large, refused to be identified with the Assamese. Even though he has made Assam his home he remains nostalgic about Calcutta. This attitude has made Bengalis unwelcome guests in all parts of the North East, be it Tripura, Assam, Meghalaya, Manipur or Nagaland."[4]

A colonial British officer has the following opinion about the Nepalis:

> "Though small in stature these Nepalis have big hearts—naturally vigorous, excitable and aggressive, they are very law abiding"—was the remark made by L.S.S.O'Malley, the author of the *Bengal District Gazetteers*.

Similarly, the Assamese were described by Col. Shakespear as—"a peaceful, almost effeminate race, in no great number, addicted, in large number, to opium eating and not disposed to diligent labour". So the two peoples made friends easily, lived together side by side in permanent peace and harmony. The Nepalis, wherever they lived, irrespective of hills or plains, spoke the local languages, dressed like the local people and acted in the manner their neighbours did, and merged in the Indian main stream, as the time passed by. Professor A.C. Sinha, noted Social scientist, remarked:

> "Most of the residents (Nepalis) have adapted themselves to the local conditions in such a way that they are counted among the indigenous[5] people with all the benefits even though they have their own communities and their own way of life, speak their language and maintain their own tradition. But the Nepalis have a great capacity to assimilate themselves

> with the hill communities. They adopt the language of their neighbourhood, contract marital alliances and turn out to be an inseparable part of the local economy."[6]

The Nepalis participated in the local festivals and cultural activities of Assamese people like Bihu festival, Raslila, Sankar Dev/Madhab Dev Tithi, performance of Ankia Nat, Bhawana etc. Mention may be made of the active participation in dancing and singing in Bihu festivals by Nepali artists like Anju Devi, Bipul Bahadur, Chandrakala Newar, Arati Pradhan, Gitanjali Chhetri etc.[7] Nepali young artist Raju Shrestha of Golaghat, Barapathar village excelled Assamese artists in Bihu dance and won prizes. He is also expert in Bihu song, Husari song and Bihunam and also plays Bihu Dhol and Pepa. Binod Khanal, another Nepali folk artiste received the Pratima Barua Pandey Memorial Award in December, 2018 for his excellent contribution to folk culture of Assam. This award which carried a citation and a cash prize of Rs. 25 thousand was sponsored by the All Assam Students Union (AASU) and was presented to him by AASU Adviser, Shri Samujjal Kumar Bhattacharya.[8] Binod Khanal has dedicated 25 years of his life in development of Nepali and Assamese folk culture and worked in various theatres across Assam including Sonam Theatre, Axomi Theatre, Bhaskar Theatre, Nataraj Theatre, Aradhana Theatre, Brahmaputra Theatre etc. Nepali youths regularly take part in the cultural shows during the Asom Sahitya Sabha Sessions. Greeting of near and dear ones with *fulam-gamosa*, usage of *Kharudaiya Japi* in the working field, entertaining guests with *Tamol-Pan Bota* or *Kharai* and wearing *Eri-chadar* in winter cold are common practices of the Nepalis in Assam. The Nepali women folk wear *Riha-mekhela chadar* while attending social function. They also join Assamese women in catching fish in the *Khal-bil* with Jakoi. Majgaon and Bahbari, two closely situated villages inhabited by Nepali and Asamiya communities since 150 years past have exhibited an exemplary assimilation of mutual cultures and languages. Assamese girls like Dipika Goswami, Dikshyamani Das and Pabitra Bhuyan of Bahbari village have earned accolades by singing beautiful Nepali songs while Nepali youths like Hemanta Timsina, Samir Pokhrel and many others of Majgaon have shown their talents by participating in Ras-Bhawna and Assamese cultural shows. In Gangmouthan (near Behali) the holy *Than* of Mahapurukh Sankardev is deeply revered by the Nepalis of that locality. One Raghubir Chhetri renovated the *Than* by removing the decayed and shrivelled thatch roof with GCI sheet. Besides taking care of the *Than,* one Nepali Brahmin offers prayers to it every day.[9] This reminds us of one Nepali Brahmin, Rati Kanta Upadhyaya by name who acted as *Satradhikar* of two *Satras*, one at Tiyak of Sibsagar and another at Nowgong which are known as *Nepali Satras* till today. This Nepali Brahmin Rati Kanta Upadhyaya so fully assimilated with Assamese culture that, Dr. Tirthanath Sarma was led to presume that the present host of Assamese *Gokhains* might be the descendants of this Nepali *Satradhikar*.

Closely following the footsteps of Rati Kanta Upadhyaya, as discussed above, another devoted Nepali, Mohanlal Upadhyaya played a significant role in propagation of Neo-Vaishnavism of Srimanta Sankar Dev. He was a dedicated Bhakta of Mahapurus Shrimanta Sankar Dev and an active member of the Sankar Sangha from 1947 to 1970. With a view to propagating Sankardev's mission he founded his own Sangha in 1971 known as Sri Sri Sankardeb Prachar Sangha and took upon himself the leadership of the Sangha as its President. He preached the teachings of Sri Sankardev among the people tirelessly travelling from place to place across the state of Assam. He indoctrinated thousands of people of various communities including Nepali and established many *Namghars* in Dhemaji, Lakhimpur, Biswanath, Sonitpur, Golaghat, Morigaon, Nagaon, Karbi Anglonbg, Chaigaon etc. The Asom Sahitya Sabha published a booklet entitled "*Asamiya Nepali Samaj Aru Sanskritir Ruprekha*" in which Mohanlal Upadhyaya was described as "a whole hearted devotee of Mahapurush Srimanta Sankardev". He steered by himself the Sri Sri Sankardev Prachar Sangha as its President for 48 years, from its founding till his death in August 2018. At present the Sangha is run by a committee of three members one of which is the son of Mohanlal Upadhyaya himself. (Reference: *History and Culture of Assamese Nepali*, Government of Assam, pp. 397-98)

Impact of Assamese Language

The children of Nepalis in Assam do not go to Nepali medium schools. They study in Assamese medium schools right from Pre-primary standard to Matriculation. Except a few schools in Shillong, Gauhati, Tura and Dibrugarh there is no Nepali medium school in the whole of Brahmaputra valley of Assam. Unlike other communities such as Bengalis, Biharis and Muslims, the Nepali guardians of Assam have never felt the necessity of sending their children to Nepali medium school. They value Assamese language even more than many of the Asamiyas themselves who send their wards to English medium schools. The children of Nepalis not only communicate in Assamese language but also write letters to their parents and friends in Assamese language, because they have not learnt Nepali script. This fact has not pinched the conscience of the guardians or prompted them to establish Nepali schools for their children. It is not that they have no money to construct and maintain Nepali school: they have constructed many Assamese schools and colleges for their children and donated generously to such schools. For example, in 1941 Chabilal Upadhyaya established Behali High School in the Nepali concentrated area which is running till today but he never asked for introducing Nepali medium in that school. Devi Prasad Pokhrel donated Rs. 40,000 to Behali High School, Brihaspati Upadhyaya donated Rs. 20,000 to Hari Mandir, Prabhuram Karki donated Rs. 5,000 to Darrang College and Prasad Singh Subba donated his land to Netra Milon Chhetra. A number of educational institutions were built up in various parts of Assam with the financial help and efforts of Nepalis like, Bhim Bahadur Vidyapith (MV School), Buda Chapari M.E. School, Behali MV School, Prajapati Rijal Higher Secondary School, Gamiri, Shingari, Nikasi, Sholong, Lekhapani, Purbanchal High School etc. The hard earned money of these Nepalis by selling milk and paddy, jute and sugarcane etc. go for the construction of Assamese school buildings with a sense of missionary zeal and enthusiasm. Recently in the wake of New Education Policy which prescribes schooling of children in mother tongue up to standard five many communities like Bodo, Kachari, Assamese etc. have demanded introduction of mother tongue in schools for their children but the Nepalis have opted for Assamese language. This was stated by Mr. Ranose Pegu, Minister of Education, Assam.

The palpable result of this secular attitude of these broad minded Nepali Mahajans, was the emergence of a large scale pro-Asamiya Nepali educated youths who were the future builders of Assam. There cropped up a good number of Nepali youths educated in Assamese schools who become doctors, engineers, lawyers, professors etc. and they turned out to be the proud assets and future builders of Assam. The Assamese language became the common medium of expression of them which so permeated into the daily conversation among the Nepalis that many Assamese words crept into Nepali colloquial vocabulary. A few of them are given below.

Nepali	Assamese	Corrupted Nepali
Kera	Kal	Kol
Bhui Katar	Anaras	Anaras
Ukhu	Kuhiyar	Kuier
Inar/Kup	Kuwa	Kuwa
Dailo	Darja	Darja
Jhyal	Khiriki	Khirki
Pul	Dalang	Dolong
Dunga	Naw	Naw
Supari	Tamol	Tamal
Chiya	Shah	Cha
Besar	Haladi	Haldi
Kaag	Kauri	Kaurhi
Utranu	Namaa	Namnu
Charhnu	Uthaa	Uthnu
Piunu	Khowa	Khanu

Nepalis Contribution to Assamese Literature

The Nepalis of Assam not only spoke Assamese fluently but also wrote stories and novels and composed poems in Assamese language. A significant result of the adoption of Assamese medium of education by the Nepalis was the emergence a number of Nepali litterateurs who wrote books, articles and poems in Assamese language and contributed to the development of Assamese literature. Trailokya Bhattarcharya wrote in the *Khadiniya Khangbad* dated 23-1-1992 as follows—

> "..... these people (Nepalis) who can speak Assamese so fluently as to put an Asamiya to shame, are writing in Assamese. One of them who secured the

> highest marks in Assamese language in his Degree examination is publishing his Assamese translation of the Act (drama) *Mukhyamantri* through the pages of this journal."

The poems, short stories and travelogues written by Hari Prasad Gorkha Rai and Dhan Bahadur Sonar in pure Assamese have occupied proud place in Assamese literature. The Government of Assam awarded literary pension of Rs. 600 per month to Hari Prasad Gorkha Rai in recognition of his contribution to Assamese literature. Today, the Nepalis living in Assam have the right to be proud of those Nepali writers who have contributed their precious little to the Assamese literature with their writings: to name some of the writers—Bishnulal Upadhyaya, Poet Haribhakta Katowal, Abinash Shrestha, Puspalal Upadhyaya, Man Bahadur Chhetri, Hari Gajurel, Agni Bahadur Chhetri, Padma Dhakal, Tarapati Updhyaya, Geeta Devi Upadhyaya, Indra Kanta Karki, Sada Dahal, Lakshmi Parajuli, Durbasa Upadhyaya etc. Two Nepali Sahitya Academi awardees, Lil Bahadur Chhetri and poet Puspalal Upadhyaya have made Assam proud by their excellent works, *Brahmaputrako Chew-chaw* and *Ushamanjari*. The river Brahmaputra has not only been the life-line of the Nepalis from where they earn their livelihood but also the creative source of the Nepali literature. Many poems, short stories and dramas have been written on river Brahmaputra. They have a monthly magazine named "Brahmaputra" which itself reflects their regard for the river. The Assamese intelligentsia in particular and the people of Assam in general have not failed to acknowledge the great contribution made by these Nepali writers. The Asom Sahitya Sabha at its Dhubri Session duly felicitated Hari Prasad Gorkha Rai and took to publish the drama of Rup Konwar Jyoti Prasad Agarwala, Karengar Ligiri translated into Nepali by Smt. Geeta

Upadhyaya and the article entitled—*Nepalis of Assam and their Culture* written in Assamese by Man Bahadur Chhetri. Bishnulal Upadhyay's "Mahapurukh Sankardev" and "Dugaraki Mahan Bibhuti" written in Assamese shows his profound love and regards for Assamese language, literature and culture. The great contribution made by Nepalis to Assamese literature has not gone unnoticed or unappreciated by Assamese intelligentsia. The noted journalist and social activist of Assam, Shri Homen Bargohain wrote the following lines in his Good will Message to the Nepali souvenir *Shailaputri* published from Majgaon in 2012 to commemorate hundred years of Durga Puza:

> "During the last one hundred years the Nepalis living in Assam have played a significant and historic role in the formation of a new Asamiya race by integration with various tribes and communities of Assam. The Nepali community being itself a peaceful and culturally conscious race has not only preserved and protected its own culture and language but also has greatly contributed to the development of Assamese language, culture and national pride. I myself feel proud to recollect the fact that I had received my first lesson in Assamese language from none other than a Nepali teacher. He was late Chandralal Jaishi of Gahapur. Today I take this opportunity to convey my respectful homage to him."[10]

Shri Mahim Bara, the President of the Asom Sahitya Sabha, while appreciating the Nepalis of Assam, described them as those who can be truly considered as Asamiya. He wrote in the following words:

> "those who remain close to Assamese society both during their festivities as well as their adversities, are

> the real children of mother Assam; they are the true Asamiyas."[11]

By the above words, Shri Mahim Bora meant the Nepalis of Assam who have been found together with Assamese society during their joys and sorrows, opportunities and adversities. Replying to the above monumental idea of Shri Mahim Bora, Bishnulal Upadhyaya opined with equal streak of conscience and said—

> "If the present process of 'integration' of the Nepalis with the larger Asamiya society crosses its limit to go even for a complete 'assimilation' in its own natural course, so be it; but let it not be by compulsion. To achieve this process of assimilation, it requires a liberal mindset, brotherly feeling and an ambience of missionary zeal from both sides."[12]

The above comments made by the two learned gentlemen bear a good deal of significance and truth. Shri Mahim Bora's assertion that those who remain close to Assamese in times of both festivities as well as adversities, are real Asamiyas, is a truism, there is no denying the fact. At the same time, Bishnulal Upadhyaya's comment that the mutual closeness between the two sides must grow from the heart, as a matter of course, and not by compulsion, is also a fact to be reckoned.

The foregoing paragraphs will speak loud and clear how the Nepalis have ever stood by the side of the Assamese people during various times of their social and political adversities. The Nepalis have proved their integration with Assamese race not only by adopting their culture, language and tradition but also by actively helping and co-operating with Assamese society during their social and political problems. In the following paragraphs we shall discuss about the Nepalis integration with the greater Assamese race in times of their national hardships.

'Save the Assamese Race'

On 28 November, 1937 when Pandit Nehru visited Rangiya, Ambika Giri Rai Choudhury and Nilamani Phukan submitted a memorandum to him on behalf of *Asamiya Samrakshini Sabha* which, among other things, states as follows:

> "... as a means of **saving the Assamese race** from extinction, a considerable section of the Assamese intelligentsia have even expressed their minds in favour of the secession of Assam from India. This is how the present situation appears to the average Assamese, and they look to you, the National Congress, to help the Assamese to get out of these dangers."[13]

The above situation occurred in colonial Assam due to continuous and heavy influx of Muslims into Assam from East Bengal and Sylhet for several decades. The immigration of Bengali speaking Muslims into Assam began right from 1874 when the district of Sylhet was tagged with Assam and Assam was created a new Chief Commissioners province. At that time, the Assamese people did not feel the influx of Muslims from Sylhet, as there was plenty of waste lands in Assam and the newcomers helped grow more food for Assam. In 1905, Assam was merged with East Bengal to become a new province called Eastern Bengal and Assam with its new capital at Dacca instead of Shillong. As a result of strong protest by both Assamese and Bengali people after six years, in 1911 Assam was again separated from East Bengal and restored to its original position with capital at Shillong. During this period of six years there was heavy influx of land hungry Bengali Muslims from East Bengal to Assam. The Muslims continued to flow unabated even after 1911—from the densely populated areas of East Bengal to the scarcely populated pockets of Assam. For example—in 1911 the number of Muslim population was 3,65,540, it rose to 5,95,981 in 1921 and in 1931 it shot up to 9,53,299 (*Political History of Assam*, Vol. II, edited by A.C. Bhuyan and Sibopado De, Government of Assam, 1978: 308).

The Muslim League Ministry of Assam led by Saadulla, adopted the policy of increasing Muslim population in Assam by means of large scale import of them under the camouflage of "Grow more food". Large number of landless immigrants from East Bengal of whom 85 per cent were Muslims were given settlement of waste land on line system. According to an estimate in 1924 in Nowgong district a total of 1619 Muslim familes were settled with waste land. The Assamese people's fear of being swamped away by outsiders began as early as 1920s. Ambikagiri Rai Choudhury formed Asamiya Samrakshini Sabha in 1926 to arouse awareness for saving Assamese. The publication of Census Report in 1931 revealing the existence of overwhelming number of Muslim population in Assam shocked the conscience of the Assamese intelligentsia. C.S. Mullan, the then Superintendent of Census 1931 wrote as follows about the invasion by the "immigrant army":

> "...(the Muslims) has almost completed the conquest of Nowgong. The Barpeta Sub-division of Kamrup has also fallen to their attack and Darrang is being invaded. Sibsagar has so far escaped completely, but the few thousand Mymensinghias in North Lakhimpur are an outpost which, may during next decade, prove to be a valuable basis for major operations. Wheresoever the carcass, there the vultures be gathered together; where there is wasteland thither flock the Mymensinghias" (Census Report, 1931-51).

An article published by Jagannath Bora in "Dainik Batori" in 1937 further cautioned the Assamese people. He wrote—unless Sylhet is separated from Assam; unless Assamese is made the state language of Assam, and unless influx of East Bengal Muslims is stopped it would be difficult for Assamese people to survive as a nationality.[14]

Thus, driven by the fear of becoming strangers in their own home land and the danger of Assam being included into Pakistan, Ambikagiri Rai Choudhury beseeched, in a printed leaflet, the tribals, the Nepalis and the tea garden labourers to save Assam and Assamese race. He requested them to return their mother tongue as Assamese in the 1941 census. In a largely attended public meeting organised at Majgaon (Behali) Natya Mandir in 1941 under the chairmanship of Chabilal Upadhyaya, Ambikagiri Rai Choudhury requested all Nepalis and teatribe Adhibasis to return their mother tongue as Assamese, their religion as Hindu and their community as Assamese before the census enumerators for the greater interest of the Assamese nation. In return to this, he assured of giving them all the political, economic and national rights in Assam as those enjoyed by the Assamese themselves."[15]

The Nepalis of Assam rose to the occasion and in large number returned their mother tongue as Assamese before the enumerators in 1941 census. Under the leadership of Chhabilal Upadhyaya, the Nepali Congress workers throughout Assam instructed the Nepalis to enumerate their mother tongue as Assamese. In this way, the Nepalis of Assam stood by the side of Assamese people at time of their distress. The Nepalis continued this practice of returning their mother tongue as Assamese even during the later census also.

The Grouping Plan and Assam

In 1946, a Cabinet Mission consisting of Lord Pathick Lawrence, Sir Stufford Cripps and A.V. Alexander arrived India with a plan to allow full scale self-government to India. For this purpose, the Cabinet Mission proposed to group provinces into three groups—A, B and C, which were to include provinces such as Bombay, the Punjab, the North West Frontier, Bengal and Assam states that had a mixed religious compositions. The Cabinet mission had cleverly clubbed Assam with Muslim majority Bengal under group-C with a view to creating a Muslim dominated zone so that when the question of partition comes up, the group-C, i.e. (Bengal and Assam) can be included in Pakistan.

This Grouping Plan of the Cabinet Mission was strongly opposed by the people of Assam and demonstrated their resentment. All schools and colleges were closed and the students came out to the streets. Hartals, demonstrations and processions were observed at Tezpur, Gahapur, Golghat and many other places. At this critical juncture of Assam, the Nepalis living in various parts of Assam joined hands with Assamese people in putting up their combined protest. The 4th General Conference of the All India Gorkha League held at Tezpur in April, 1947 adopted resolution strongly protesting against M.A. Jinna's "Two Nations" theory. The resolution demanded abolition of the Grouping Plan and made it clear that if it is necessary thirty lakhs Khukuris would be used to defend the interest of Assam.[16]

The voices of protest and rejection were raised across the country. In Punjab the Sikh and the Hindus protested against the plan for fear of being dominated by the Muslims whose population was bigger. Nirode Baruah called the Cabinet Mission Plan a "sinister" plan. Gopinath Bordoloi, Chief

Minister of Assam warned the Central leaders that the Assamese people would consider it as a "great betrayal" if they impose the Cabinet Mission plan on them. Although Nehru supported the plan Mahatma Gandhi strongly opposed it. Sardar Patel also backed the Assamese and wrote to Stafford Cripps stating that Grouping plan was a betrayal. The British Government finally realised that the plan could not be thrust upon the Assamese people against their will. So the plan was abandoned and the crisis was averted. Thus, Assam was saved from being included in Pakistan.

Contribution of Gorkha Soldiers

The supreme sacrifice of life made by the Gorkha soldiers, for Assam in particular and India in general, cannot be overlooked. In 1826, the Gorkhas expelled the Burmese from Assam valley, quelled the Moamoriah rebellion, and subdued the war-like hill tribes and brought back peace and order. The Gorkhas saved the Assamese people from Burmese atrocities. Taking the advantage of political turmoil, the Burmese had overran the country of Assam unleashing a reign of terror, with barbaric plunder, kidnapping and murder. "Thirty thousand Assamese had been carried off as slaves by the Burmese. Many thousands had lost their lives and large tracts of country been laid desolate by the wars, famines and pestilences."[17] Gunabhiram Baruah (1834–1894) estimated a population of Assam to be 2.5 million before 1,76,018. Assam, in the words of Anandaram Dhekial Phukan, a noted Assamese Government official, "groaned under the oppression and lawless tyranny of the Burmese", that destroyed more than half of the Assamese population. At such distressful juncture, the Gorkhas of the British force, emerged as the Messiah, the saviour of the Assamese people.[18] The Gorkhas brought peace not only in the Brahmaputra valley but also in the entire North East frontier including the hill areas and forged a unification of a greater Assam. Professor A.C. Sinha rightly said—

> "The Nepalese did contribute in the integration, consolidation, development and reconstruction of the Indian state, especially the North-eastern states, a point which should not be forgotten."[19]

During the Chinese aggression in October, 1962, the Chinese troops descended from Thag La ridge in overwhelming number and mounted a massive attack supported by field artillery and mortars and easily overran the Indian posts. They crossed the Mac Mohan Line in other sectors also and launched offensives against Indian posts located in NEFA areas. The Gorkhas of the 9th G.R. and Assam Rifles bore the brunt of first attacks completely unprepared. At Khenzemane, the Chinese attacked three Indian posts at 04.00 hours of 20 October with heavy bombardment by field guns and mortars. The Gorkhas fought valiantly for nearly two hours but the overwhelmingly superior number of the Chinese troops blew away Indian post. Hav. Som Bahadur and twenty others went down fighting and got killed. Subedar Kharka Bahadur commander of the forward platoon and his men fought back valiantly killing 12 and wounding at least 15 Chinese. The gallant Gorkhas pushed them back for the second time inflicting heavy casualties. Seeing that the stubborn Gorkhas would not give them an inch, the Chinese went behind the D company and launched a rear attack. Havildar Chandra Bahadur Pun, then took over the LMG and kept the enemy at bay by continuous firing from close range until the last man of his company was out of the enemy cordon. In the western Ladakh sector Major Dhansing Thapa earned the highest gallantry award, Param Veer Chakra fighting the Chinese.

The Chinese troops advanced forward and reached Bomdilla. Fearing their further advance, the Assam Government evacuated Tezpur town and burnt down the Government treasury. The tea garden managers fled their bunglows and the civilian people were at the verge of fleeing. The Nepalis did not budge at all. They remained strong and advised people to take courage and hold on, until finally normalcy and peace returned back. Manirul Hussain writes:

> "In the wake of Chinese aggression of 1962 many Nepali soldiers sacrificed their lives to protect the North East frontier India. This generated tremendous sympathy for the Nepalis in Assam. They were largely well accepted and well treated in the larger Assamese society."[20]

During the Second World War, in 1943 a large number of Gorkha soldiers joined the Indian National Army (Azad Hind Fouj) of Netaji Subhas Chandra Bose and fought against the British to liberate mother India from the colonial rule. They fought heroically in Burma in collaboration with Japanese and reached up to Imphal and Kohima. But eventually they had to withdraw. In this battle 25 Gorkha soldiers sacrificed their lives fighting in the Arakan including two martyrs, Major Durga Malla and Captain Dal Bhadur Thapa who were captured by British force, brought to Delhi and hanged to death on the 25th August, 1944 and 3rd May, 1945, after short trials.[21]

Bengali *Versus* Assamese Medium in Schools

Assam was made the Chief Commissioner's Province in 1874 and major portion of the Bengali speaking areas of Cachar and Sylhet were merged with Assam. For the administrative convenience of the Bengali Babus working in Assam, in 1836 the British authorities introduced Bengali language in the offices, courts and schools instead of Assamese language. Initially for a few years no one objected to this arrangement, but when the Baptist Missionaries started schools in Assam they raised the question of teaching medium for the indigenous children of Assam. Assamese is an Indo-Aryan language having its roots in the Sanskrit and is almost similar with Bengali. It was developing ever since 14th century when Madhab Kandali had translated *Ramayana* in Assamese language. In the later period, the Ahom kings had made it the court language, and by the time the British took over Assam it had become the lingua-franca of the Province. Therefore, it was legitimate that Assamese language be taught in schools instead of Bengali. The Assamese intelligentsia like Anandaram Dhekial Phukan, Hem Chandra Baruah, Gunabhiram Baruah etc. pleaded for the Assamese as medium of instruction and official language. In this connection they submitted a resolution adopted in Assam Hitaysini Shobha dated November, 1872 to the Lieutenant Governor of Bengal.[22] Finally in 1874 George Campbell, the Lieutenant Governor General of India replaced Assamese to its rightful place, as the medium of instruction in Assam. Still then, some influential Bengalis of Gauhati demanded for Bengali to be the medium of instruction at High School level and both Assamese and Bengali languages were being taught in schools all over Assam.

The Asom Sahitya Sabha was established in 1917 for the protection and development of Assamese language and literature. The Sabha did not limit its activities to the promotion of Assamese literature alone but had a broader objective of unifying, promoting and developing the traditions and cultures of all the indigenous Assamese people and their languages. It took up the cause of recognising Assamese as the medium of instruction in colleges and universities in the Brahmaputra valley. On 11 March, 1950, the Asom Sahitya Sabha adopted a resolution on the official language and successfully carried on a campaign in favour of Assamese as the state language. In 1959 and 1960, the Asom Sahitya Sabha consecutively adopted resolutions demanding Assamese language to be introduced as the state language of Assam. On 16 July, 1961, it observed the State Language Day in the Brahmaputra valley. The Assam Provincial Congress Committee in its resolution of April 22, 1960 reiterated the demand made by Asom Sahitya Sabha. The students of Gauhati University held demonstration before Jawaharlal Nehru, Prime Minister of India, when he came to Guwahati, demanding introduction of Assamese as official language of Assam.

Language is the most sensitive subject for which one can sacrifice even his life. The State of Assam broke into pieces to form different tribal states because of the language policy adopted by Assam government. After 1960, the introduction of Assamese as official language of Assam contributed to a large scale protest and demand for separate hill states by the hill leaders of Assam and finally the hill districts were separated from Assam to constitute six different states. Biseswar Brahma of Bodo Sahitya Sabha and Mohini Basumatari MLA were assassinated by Bodo militants because of Bodo language issue. Similar situation was created in Tripura for the safeguard of Kok Barak language. The Bengalese of Assam never yielded to the language policy of Assam Government. The Tamilians protested tooth and nails when attempts were made to enforce Hindi in Tamil Nadu during fifties. Imposition of Assamese language struck the trigger of Hill state movement. Under the background stated above, the firm support for Assamese as a medium of instruction by the Nepalis of Assam for the last more than a century must be viewed as a glaring proof of their cultural integration with larger Asamiya society.

Official Language Bill, 1960

In view of the repeated demands from Asom Sahitya Sabha, Shri B.P. Chaliha, Chief Minister of Assam introduced the Assam Official Language Bill in the Assembly on 10 October, 1960. The Bengali speaking people of Assam especially those living in Barak valley were raising their voice against introduction of Assamese language as official language. The Bengalese are known for their pride of culture, language and literature. In the matter of language their voice is always louder than any other community. This time they got the support of tribal leaders of the hills in the wake of their demand for separate Hill States. Immediately on introduction of the Assamese language bill on 10 October, 1960, the Nikhil Assam Banga Bhasha Samiti was formed with Negendra Chandra Shyam as its President for the purpose of protesting against the Bill. The Nikhil Assam Banga Bhasha Samiti together with Cachar Jila Gana Sangram Parishad intensified their protest against the Bill. The protest was actively supported by the Calcutta University Students Union and many political leaders from West Bengal. The Hill leaders of Khasi and Jaintia Hills and Garo Hills joined the protest while Captain W.A. Sangma who was the Minister of Education, Assam resigned his office demanding separate Hill State. The Bengalis formed Bhasa Andolan Samiti throughout Cachar district and launched demonstrations, *hartals, Padayatra, Satyagraha* and all forms of protests—a few of them turning into violent mobs, burning and destroying public properties and clashing with Police.

In such situation, the Nepali community stood firm by the side of the Government of Assam in support of Assamese language. Their MLA, Bishnulal Upadhyaya, speaking in the House of the Assam Assembly strongly supported the passing of the Bill. Chhabilal Upadhyaya made a statement saying that one who live in Assam must speak Assamese and they must send their children to Assamese schools. He stated that, unlike Bengalis the Nepalis guardians in Assam have been not only sending their children in Assamese medium schools but also constructing Assamese school buildings and donating money for construction of Assamese medium schools and colleges for their children. Finally, the Bill was passed on 24 October. It received Governor's assent on 17 December, 1960 and was published in the *Assam Gazette* on 19 December, 1960. The Section 3 of the Act provided that Bengali language shall continue to be used for administrative purposes in Cachar district until the Mahakuma Parishad and the Municipal Board of the district, in a joint meeting decided in favour of Assamese language being voted by not less than two-thirds of members present. Thus, the Nepalis have always taken the side of the Assamese people in any of their cause.

The passing of the Bill was severely resented and protested by Bengalese and also by many tribal people of Khasi and Jaintia Hills, Garo Hills, Naga and Mizo Hills etc. Demonstrations, *Hartals* and Bandhs continued to be held by Bengali students in the Barak valley. On 19 May, 1961, a procession taken out by students and the public took a turn towards violence when it reached near the Silchar Railway station. The police had to *lathi* charge and then open fire to control the violent mob which resulted in the death of eleven people including one woman.

Assam Movement

The Assam movement was one of the epoch making events in the history of Assam. This movement was sponsored by the All Assam Students Union (AASU) and the All Assam Gana Sangram Parishad (AAGSP) in 1979 which continued for long six years and ended on 15 August, 1985 with the signing of an agreement between the Government of India and the student bodies which is known as the Assam Accord. The prime objective of this movement was to make Assam free of foreign infiltrators, i.e.—the illegal Bangladeshis. This was an agitation to bring home to the Government of India the fact of large scale illegal immigration of people from Bangladesh and to compel the Government to identify and expel those infiltrators through due process of law. The Assamese people as a whole was in the fear of being minority in their own homeland and being swamped away by the foreigners. The student bodies who waited for long and having exhausted all means had to take recourse to this extreme step to save the Assamese race and to secure to the indigenous people their legal and constitutional rights. The agitation though, at the beginning, was intended to be a non-violent movement, however towards the end took a turn to arson and killing culminating in the massacre of thousands of lives.

The Nepalis living in Assam were also the targets of the Assam movement although, at the beginning Nepali youths also had joined hands with Assamese students and took active part in the movement. The Nepali boys sacrificed their lives too for the cause of Assamese people. Out of the 860 Assamese boys who became martyrs during the Assam movement, there were six Nepali youths who also became martyrs for the sake of Assam. As the true sons of the soil, they were imbued with the sense of love for the mother Asom. During action they breathed their last by uttering—*Jai Ai Asom.* On the day of "Shraddhanjali" held at Khanapara Veterinary College playground, which was attended by many Ministers and political leaders, Sarbananda Sonowal, Chief Minister of Assam declared that Rs. 5 lakh each would be given to the nearest kins of the martyrs. The Nepali community of Assam feel proud of the six Nepali youths who sacrificed their lives for the sake of mother Assam and offer their hearty *Shraddhanjali* to them. The names and addresses together with serial numbers of the six Nepali martyrs, as appeared in the epitaph erected at Khanapara play ground, are given below:

1. Dhan Bahadur Chhetri, Boko, Kamrup (Sl. 45)
2. Kul Bahadur Chhetri, Silapathar, Lakhimpur (Sl. 182)
3. Padma Bahadur Chhetri, Amguri, Lakhimpur (Sl.187)
4. Khirod Bahadur Tamang, Uttar Salmara, Goalpara (Sl. 446)
5. Baijayanti Devi, Charduar, Tezpur (Sl. 633)
6. Bhim Bahadur Tamang, Gahapur, Viswanath (Sl. 727)

Citizenship Amendment Act, 2019 (CAA)

The Citizenship (Amendment) Bill (CAB) 2019, despite mass peoples protest against it throughout Assam, was passed by the Indian Parliament on the 11th December, 2019. The Citizenship Amendment Act, 2019 seeks to amend the Citizenship Act, 1955 in order to provide citizenship rights and to protect certain persons from proceedings of illegal migration. According to Citizenship Amendment Act, 2019, persons belonging to Hindu, Sikh, Buddhist, Jain, Parsi and Christian communities who have migrated to India before 31 December, 2014 after facing persecution on grounds of religion in Pakistan, Afghanistan and Bangladesh would be granted Indian citizenship. The Bharatiya Janata Party (BJP) which is in power of the Government passed this Bill in order to fulfil its promises made during the past election manifesto, despite strong protest made by more than half of the states in India. The people all over the country, especially from Assam opposed the Bill tooth and nail leading to police firing on the protesters and killing a few people. The opposition parties protested the Bill on the ground that religion had been overtly used as criterion for the amendment of citizenship Bill in violation of the secular spirit of the constitution. They also charged the BJP Government for promoting its Hindu nationalistic agenda. The Office of the United Nations High Commissioner of Human Rights (OHCHR) called it "Fundamentally discriminatory". Some political leaders accused the Government for excluding similar benefits to other persecuted religious minorities from countries like Tibet, Sri Lanka and Myanmar. It violates Article 14 of the Constitution which says, "The States shall not deny to any person equality before the law, or the equal protection of the laws within the territory of India". All regional and national political parties of the North East India joined the fray in opposition of the CAA. Anti-CAA sentiment found echoes in Churches too. Some regional dioceses of the Catholic Church of India declared January 26, the 71st Republc Day celebration as Constitution Protection Day. Even some of the MLAs and MPs of the BJP itself from the North East expressed their opposition to the Bill. Fearing a setback in the ensuing Lok Sabha election Home Minister, Amit Shah exempted the application of the provisions of the Citizenship Amendment Bill in the hill states of North East except Tripura and Sikkim. The people of Assam protested tooth-and-nail against the CAA for fear of being swamped away by the Hindu Bengalese from Bangldesh who were staying illegally in Assam in great number. In Barak valley of Assam, the Bengalese have already outnumbered the Assamiyas where Bengali language is the official language and Bengali culture is predominant. The Assamese, therefore, had reason to believe that their only stronghold, the Brahmaputra valley too might be turned into Barak valley if the Hindu Bengalis from Bangladesh are granted citizenship.

The Nepalis of Assam came forward to join hands with the agitating Assamese people. They paraded the streets and demonstrated together with the Assamese people. Prem Tamang, President of the Gorkha Students Union (GSU) joined the band-wagon with his followers. The Gorkhas under the banner of Assam Gorkha Sammelan (AGS) and the Bharatiya Gorkha Parisangha (BGP) re-iterated their strong opposition to the Citizenship Amendment Act, 2019 and threatened to come out with their *Khukuris* unless Assam is exempted from the purview of the Act.[23] Explaining their demand for exemption of entire Assam from the purview of the CAA, Bhaskar Dahal, General Secretary of the Assam Gorkha Sammelan said—"The Act will invite threat to the indigenous Gorkhas of Assam who are constituent of the greater Assamese society. This Act if not exempted now, will not only change the demography of Assam, but will also adversely affect the official Assamese language, the community's cultural assimilation, art, literature, and finally will lead to challenging the constitutional protection of the new settlers as committed in the Assam Accord. Nitya Nanda Upadhyaya, President of the Bharatiya Gorkha Parisangh (Assam State) said—"The Assam Accord is a national commitment by the Government of India to the people of Assam; Clause Six of Assam Accord which guarantees constitutional protection of the indigenous communities should be implemented even before the Act is notified nationwide, exempting Assam and the North East."[24]

Nepalis Population is 'Negligible' in Assam

The Nepali population in Assam is 'negligible' when compared to the total population. The percentage of Nepalis population in Assam according to 2001 Census was a miniscule of 2.12 per cent to the total population of the state. Table 3.1 shows the population and percentages of major communities of Assam, *vis-à-vis* the Nepalis to the total population of the state.

Table 3.1 shows that Nepalis population of 2.12 per cent to the total population of Assam is a negligible number compared to Bengali population of 27.66 per cent and also other communities. The Bengali population with 27.66 per cent was the highest among outsiders followed by 5.88 per cent of the Hindustanis and the Nepalis the lowest with 2.12 per cent. Despite the facilities of free border crossing and the provisions of equal privileges in the matter of residence, ownership of property, participation in trade and commerce, movement and other privileges made available to Nepalese nationals by the treaty of 1950, the migration of Nepalese into Assam remained a very small number. For this reason, according to Manirul Hussain, the protest against the Nepalese migration to Assam has never been strong even during the Assam movement.[25] The Nepalis population in Assam is so small (2.12%) that the dominant section of the Asamiya does not consider the Nepalis as an emerging threat to their middle class monopoly, unlike the Bemgalis and Hindustanis in Assam. The Nepalis of Assam are, at present, in no position to threaten the Asamiya middle class.[26] Sivnath Barman remarked that numerically the Nepalis are insignificant as compared to the Bengalis in Assam hence, there is less vociferosity against the Nepalis.[27] Even in the entire North East region, the Nepali population amounts to only 6,53,255 in 1991 census.

Table 3.1: Showing the percentages of major communities to the total population of Assam in 2001 census

Communities	Population	Percentage to total population
Assamese	1,31,68,484	48.84
Bengali	73,43,388	27.66
Hindi	15,69,662	5.88
Bodo	12,96,162	4.86
Nepali	5,64,790	2.12
Mishing	5,06,129	1.9

Source: Census Report, 2001.

Nepalis are Economically non-contender to Locals

Economically, the Nepalis population in the North East India can be grouped under three categories, *viz.*, the retired army personnel, the children of ex-servicemen and the civilian Nepalis. The first group included the army ex-service Gorkhas who settled down in the North East after retirement, and live on their pension; the second category included the family and children of ex-army men who enjoy the pension and other facilities of their fathers or husbands; and the third category comprised the rest of the Nepalis civilian population and they are the largest economically working group. They work as farmers, herdsmen, traders, lumbermen, service men and as unskilled labour. Ninety per cent of them never contest with the local people in their economic pursuits, nor do they hamper in their social or political life in any way. Economically they are not rivals to Assamese but complementary to their economic pursuits. They never contest for government jobs, nor become rivals in any contract or business. They have no political parties or organisations nor do they demand a separate Gorkhaland or Autonomous Council. They have not joined any political insurgency or militant outfit. They are simple and law abiding people and live, by and large, in the interior villages, nooks and corners, take to cattle rearing or till the land to produce milk and food for the growing population. In the Brahmaputra valley, the Nepalis are mostly settled in, Darrang, Kamrup, Goalpara, Nowgong, Sibsagar, Manipur and North-Lakhimpur districts while in the hill areas they are there in Khasi and Jaintia Hills, Garo Hills, Naga Hills, Lushai Hills, North Kachar Hills and the North Eastern Frontier Agency (NEFA). Journalist, Sekhar Gupta wrote about Nepalis as follows:

> "Another small group of immigrants which has stubbornly refused to follow the laws of nature, were

> the Nepalis who now number about half a million. But since they stayed in their own small pockets away from population centres and did not show any proclivity for economic development, they did not prove such an irritant. The Bengalis were the strongest contender of Assamese people in every sphere of activities."[28]

The intelligentsia of Assam have, by and large, considered Nepalis as "Assamese in every way", as they have seen how the Nepalis have integrated themselves with the Asamiya society by adopting their language, culture and tradition and joining hands in their social, cultural and political struggles. In this context Dr. Maheswar Neog, noted historian and President of the Assam Sahitya Sabha, has remarked. Delivering his Presidential address in the General Conference of the Assam Sahitya Sabha, Dr. Maheswar Neog read out the following passage about the Nepalis of Assam:

> "The relation of Assam with Nepal is very old. The Assam's Nepalese are Assamese in every way. These Nepali Assamese have been joining the agitations and movements of the local people such as the Independence movement, the agitation against Grouping, the Assam Samrakshini Sabha, the activities of the Sankar Sangha and the movements for the establishment of Assamese language as the official language of Assam and as the medium of higher education here."[29]

Thus, the above words of Dr. Maheswar Neog—"the Assam's Nepalese are Assamese in every way", summarises the whole perception of Assamse people about the Nepalis and puts a naught on all speculations.

Mistaken Identity

The Nepalis living in India for generations are known by two names—Nepali and Gorkha. To an Indian the two terms 'Nepali' and 'Gorkha' are confusing and difficult to make out as to who is a Nepali or who is a Gorkha. In Indian context both the names definitely mean a person from Nepal. This situation led to a mistaken identity of the Nepalis living permanently in the North East as they were often considered to be Nepalese nationals (foreigners) by the local people who hardly bothered to know if they were Indian citizens. For, they speak the same Nepali language and look similar in every way. The Indian Nepalis are thus clubbed together with the Nepalese nationals who have come freshly from Nepal and are living in India. They are deprived of various legal and constitutional rights and benefits by the Government. They withheld their voting rights, denied Government contracts and leases and even slapped with quit India notices. What is most unacceptable is that, in the North East the Nepalis who are genuine citizens of India are treated as foreigners (Bangladeshis) and frequently mal-treated. They are assaulted, looted, even killed and their houses burnt down by the local indigenous people. They have become victims of ethnic violence in their hands during Assam Movement in 1979-85, in Manipur in 1980, in Meghalaya in 1987 and in Bodoland BTC areas in 1993.

Ever since then the Nepalis of the North East, and for that matter, of India as a whole have been facing a deep identity crisis, as commented by Professor A.C. Sinha and Dr. T. Subba. The quest for an identity that will differentiate the Gorkhas/Nepalis (Indian citizens) from the newcomer Nepalese nationals has assumed an utmost necessity. The immediate need is to find out a suitable nomenclature for Indian Gorkhas that will distinguish them from the Nepalese nationals so that the local people would not mistake them to be foreigners and perpetrate atrocities on them. There has been, therefore, a sustained effort on the part of elite Nepalis to find out a consensus nomenclature by which they could be instantly recognized as Indian citizens; so that they could feel themselves safe with dignity and honour, like—"when the mind is without fear, the head is held high" and when justice, liberty, equality and fraternity are secured to every Indian Nepali as is available to other Indians.

Demand for Abrogation of Indo-Nepal Treaty, 1950

The Article 7 of the Indo-Nepal Treaty of Peace and Friendship, 1950 allows the people of India and Nepal to cross the Indo-Nepal border freely without passport and visa and to avail equal privileges in the matter of residence, ownership of property, participation in trade and commerce, movement and other privileges of similar nature by the nationals of both the countries. Taking this advantage large number of Nepalese nationals came to the North East every year to earn their livelihood, of whom some went back to Nepal and others stayed back for a temporary settlement. According to census reports, the entry of Nepalis into Assam during the two decades of 1951 to 1961 and 1961 to 1971 was the highest ever registering the decadal growths at 112 per cent and 62 per cent respectively. The Nepalis presence in the North East caused heart-burn to the local people and often recourse to ethnic violence in order to drive them out of Assam.

Many times, the local people confused or took the permanently settled Nepalis to be newcomers from Nepal and harassed them in various ways. They called the Indian Nepalis foreigners, deleted their names from voter list, and deprived them of their economic and political rights. They were looked upon as unwanted intruders into their homes, and were victimized, threatened, assaulted, killed and, at times, uprooted from their hearths and homes. During Assam movement (1979–85) thousands of Nepalis living permanently in Assam and Manipur were driven out. Same thing happened with the Nepalis of Khasi Hills in 1987. Thus, the Indian Nepalis who are the genuine citizens of India had to suffer unnecessarily because of the influx of Nepalese nationals from Nepal.

For the reasons stated above the Nepalis living permanently in the North East do not want any fresh Nepalese nationals to come to Assam to cause unnecessary problems for them. In this context, the Assam Gorkha Sammelan, the only representative body of the Indian Nepalis living in the North East, requested the Government of India to abrogate the Article 7 of the Indo-Nepal Treaty of Peace and Friendship,1950 and to introduce Permit system which will help identification and deportation of newcomers. The Artile 7 of the Treaty of Peace and Friendship 1950 allows the people of India and Nepal to cross the border freely without passport and visa and allows the same privileges to both peoples in the matter of residence, ownership of property, participation in trade and commerce, movement and other privileges of similar nature. In this connection, a delegation consisting of eight leaders of the Assam Gorkha Sammelon including four MLAs, met the Prime Minister of India, Mrs. Indira Gandhi on the 1st February,1980 and submitted a Memorandum to her indicating all the problems faced by the Indian Nepalis living in the North East as Indian citizens and urging upon her to look into their problem at an early date.[30] They demanded that the Indo-Nepal Peace Treaty of 1950 should be suitably amended so as to ban free crossing of India-Nepal border by people of both countries. They also submitted similar memorandum to the Prime Minister of Nepal explaining their problems and difficulties and requesting him to take up the issue with Government of India and make such arrangement so as to stop free entry of Nepalese nationals into the North East region. Perhaps, nowhere on earth exist a system of free crossing of border between two sovereign countries. It is an anachronism to allow continuance of such a system which existed during British rule.

NOTES

1. Manirul Hussain (1993). *The Assam Movement*, p. 260.
2. *Ibid.*, p. 260.
3. Amalendu Guha (2006). *Planters Raj to Swaraj*, p. 170.
4. Sekhar Gupta (1984). *A Valley Divided*, Vikash Publishing House, New Delhi, p. 129.
5. Bishnulal Upadhyaya (2004). *Khanmihali* (in Assamese), Tezpur, p. 40.
6. A.C. Sinha (1990). "The Indian North East Frontier and Nepali Immigrants". In *Himalayan Environment and Culture,* N.K. Rustomji and Charles Ramble (eds.), New Delhi, p. 236.
7. Bishnulal Upadhyaya (2014). *Khanmihali*, Tezpur.
8. *Sentinel*, dated 28 December, 2018.
9. *Ibid.*, p. 39.
10. Homen Bargohain (2012). "Goodwill Message", in *Sailaputri* Nepali Souvenir, Edited Uma Pokhrel.
11. *Viswanath Dipika*, Souvenir of the 56th Conference of the Asom Sahitya Sabha, held at Viswanath Charali in 1990.
12. *Ibid.*, *Khanmihali*, p. 42.
13. Amalendu Guha (1988). *Planters Raj to Swaraj*, Reprint, p. 257.
14. *Ibid.*, p. 172.
15. P. Bhandari (1996). *Freedom Movement and the Role of Indian Nepalis*, pp. 101-103.
16. *Political History of Assam*, Published by Government of Assam.
17. *Ibid.*, p. 7.
18. Bhuyan, *Anglo-Assamese Relations,* p. 128.
19. *Ibid.,* A.C. Sinha.
20. Manirul Hussain (1993). *The Assam Movement*, p. 260.
21. P.N. Chopra (1969). *Who is Who of the Indian Martyrs*, Vol. I.

22. *Petition for recognition of Assamese Language*/General/Education, November, 1872, Proceeding No. 30-38. (From West Bengal State Archives)
23. *Telegraph*, 22-12-2019, *Gorkhas Threaten to Protest with Khukuri.*
24. *Ibid.*
25. Manirul Hussain (1993). *The Assam Movement,* p. 260.
26. *Ibid.*, p. 261.
27. Sivnath Barman (1980). *Svadesh Svamat* (in Asamiya), Chetna Prakash, Guwahati.
28. *Op cit.*, Sekhar Gupta, p. 130.
29. Bishnulal Upadhyaya (1984). *Asame Nepaliharu* (Enlarged edn.)
30. *Ibid.*, pp. 240-41.

4

The Predicaments of the Nepalis in Assam

The Nepalis have been living in Assam in close relations with the local people socially, culturally, economically and politically, for more than two hundred years. They have adopted Assamese culture and tradition and fully integrated with Assamese culture but still then they are facing certain nagging predicaments. The citizenship and voting rights of the Nepalis in Assam has continued to be questioned at different times by the Government offices despite the Indian Nepalis have been granted the citizenship rights under the Constitution of India and the Indian Citizenship Act, 1955. As per existing laws of the land, the following mentioned categories of Nepalis/Gorkhas have become automatically citizens of India and are eligible for all the civil and political rights including right to franchise on attainment of 18 years of age:

(a) Those, who were domiciled in India at the commencement of constitution, i.e., on 26-1-1950. [Under Article 5(c) of constitution]
(b) Those, who are born in India. (Under Sec. 3 of Indian Citizenship Act, 1955),

(c) Those, either of whose parents were born in India. (Under Sec. 4 of Indian Citizenship Act, 1955), and
(d) Those who are wives of the Gorkha citizens of India.

But despite the above legal provisions, the Indian Gorkhas are being harassed by the officers of Assam Governments, on many occasions by depriving them their right to exercise votes. At times, the Deputy Commissioners/Sub-Divisional Officers of some Districts/Sub-Divisions instructed the Gorkhas to obtain Indian citizenship before they were allowed to cast votes, and at others, some Election offices struck out their names from the voter lists without giving an opportunity to prove their citizenship rights. For example:

In 1960 H.N. Bora, the Deputy Commisioner of Garo Hills by his letter No. 72/60/5 dated 2-9-1960 informed all the Gorkhas in Garo Hills that merely on the ground of living for many years in India, they cannot be considered as the citizens of India unless and until they obtain Indian citizenship certificate as per Article 5 of the Constitution of India. Anybody who wanted to include his name in the voter list must get citizenship certificate as per rules mentioned above. The gist of the letter No. 72/60 dated 2 September, 1960 from Shri H.N. Borah, Deputy Commissioner, Garo Hills (Election Branch) Tura is given below:

> "It is notified for general information that the Nepalis who cannot claim Indian citizenship under Article 5 of the constitution cannot automatically become Indian citizens merely by long and continuous residence in India. These Nepalis will have to acquire Indian citizenship first under the relevant section of the Citizenship Act, 1955 before their names can be registered in the electoral rolls of the constituency in which they are residing.

> The names of some Nepalis residing in this district had been enrolled as voters in the electoral rolls of the constituencies and they were given the rights to exercise their franchise in the general election to the state Legislative, House of People and District Council as well during the years 1952 and 1957. In accordance with the provisions of law, no one but citizens of India can be enrolled in the electoral rolls and allow to exercise his franchise.
>
> Therefore, all Nepalis who wished to include their names in the electoral rolls should first acquire Indian citizenship and those whose names have been enrolled in the electoral rolls must acquire Indian citizenship now or their names will be struck off the electoral rolls".

In this case, a prompt action was taken by MLA Bishnulal Upadhyaya by putting up Assembly Question No. 246(b) which yielded positive result by setting the wrong, aright. As per order of the Chief Minister of Assam, all the DCs and SDOs were sent circulars by the Chief Electoral Officer of Assam explaining the correct position and instructing them to go by the electoral rolls of 1957. Thereafter, the D.C. Tura never raised the question of citizenship certificate and allowed the Gorkhas of Garo Hills to participate in the election.

In another case, during the 1971 mid-term election to Lok Sabha seat for Dibrugarh constituency, names of 4500 bonafide Nepali voters were deleted from the Electoral Roll without giving an opportunity to show cause. This matter caused a wide sense of resentment among the Gorkhas living for generations in Sadiya, Chapakhowa, Chunpara, Jonai and Dhola areas. A delegation under the leadership of Shri Bishnulal Upadhyaya, MLA met shri Mahendra Mohan Choudhury, Chief Minister of Assam and requested him to cause an immediate enquiry into the mass deletion of the names of genuine citizens of India. The Chief Minister gave assurance to look into the matter, but the case remained unattended under red-tapism until the time of revision of voter list for the next general election came.

So, in view of the delaying tactic of the Government, the Nepalis of Tinsukia in a meeting attended by all the Nepali voters of Dibrugarh district, adopted a resolution which decided to file a PIL Petition in the Supreme Court of India for dispensation of immediate justice. Knowing of this move by the Nepalis, Shri Bhavani Kumar Bhuyan, IAS, Special Secretary Election, Government of Assam visited Dibrugarh on the 9th August, 1971 for enquiry, when he was handed over a copy of the memorandum of the Nepali voters of Dibrugarh submitted to the Election Commission of India by Bal Bahadur Rai, President of the Dibrugarh District Committee. Thereafter, prompt action started by the Special Secretary, Assam who visited Dibrugarh, Chapakhowa, Tinsukia, Sadiya etc. and met all the concerned D.Cs, S.D.Os, Assistant Political Officers and District Returning Officers and gave them detailed instructions for revision of electoral rolls. Accordingly, Revised Voter Lists were prepared in which the 4500 deleted names of Nepali voters were included.

Instances are also there when the Superintendent of Police issued Quit India Notices to thousands of Gorkhas to leave India within a week without prior enquiry. For example:

On the 16th October, 1979 one R.N. Mathur IPS, Superintendent of Police, district Lakhimpur, Assam served notices to twenty Nepali families of Bihpuria village to quit India within a period of two weeks from the date of the notice and not to re-enter India again. The news created a panic, fear psychosis and a sense of insecurity among the Indian Nepalis at large. On being reported the matter to the Assam Gorkha Sammelan an immediate deputation under the leadership of Bishnulal Upadhyaya, MLA, waited upon the Chief Minister of Assam and the Leader of the Assam Legislature Party, Shri J.N. Hazarika. The Chief Minister expressed surprise and annoyance at the uncalled for action of the concerned officer. He immediately darted a wireless message instructing the Superintendent of Police to stop any further action on the matter until orders were received from the Government. He assured the delegation not to worry and that all necessary action would be taken. On receipt of the wireless message, the Superintendent of Police hurriedly collected back all the copies of the notices issued by him from the villagers so as to destroy the evidence of what he did. The concerned IPS officer now came to senses that he was legally not competent enough either to question a person's citizenship right or to deport such person from India on his own accord. There is a Tribunal legally appointed and a particular law in place for the purpose of detection and deportation of a person if suspected to be a foreign national and no Government officer however powerful can take the law in his own hand. It is unfortunate that there is a tendency among the Government officers in Assam to be overenthusiastic to wield unauthorised powers against innocent people. Appropriate action could be taken against such errant if not politically motivated, officer had the higher authority opted for it. Shri J.N. Hazarika, Chief Minister, Assam in his DO Letter No.CMS-781006 dated 17 November, 1979 addressed to Shri Bishnulal Upadhyaya, MLA informed him as follows[1]:

"Dear Shri Upadhyaya,

Please refer to our discussion of 16 instant regarding alleged harassment of Indian citizens of Nepali origin in Lakhimpur district. I am arranging an enquiry about the specific instances mentioned by you. If any officer is found to have acted with mala fide intention Government will take suitable action against such delinquent officer.

With regards,
Yours Sincerely,

To
S/d J.N. Hazarika"
Shri Bishnulal Upadhyaya, MLA

Exclusion of names from NRC

The exclusion of nearly one lakh Nepalis' names from the final list of National Register of Citizenship (NRC) made the situation even more confounded for the Indian Gorkhas. The NRC list left out even the names of the grand children of the freedom fighter late Chhabilal Upadhyaya and the close relatives of the Assam Movement martyr, Jayanti Devi of Tezpur. Prominent persons like Durga Prasad Khatiwada, Sahitya Akademy awardee was marked as 'D' Voter and his name was excluded from the draft NRC. What is most unfortunate is that Shri Ganesh Kumar Limbu, sitting MLA from Borsola constituency was served with a notice to prove his citizenship. All these problems overwhelmed the Nepalis of the North East, again and again, despite their legal and constitutional status were clarified several times by the Ministry of Home Affairs, Government of India as well as the Chief Election Commissioner of India.

The Nepalis are Neglected Community

The Nepalis of Assam have been made to feel that

they are one of the most neglected communities among all the composite greater Asamiya societies. Despite the Nepalis have fully integrated with the Assamese society to be identified as indigenous tribe they are deprived of many benefits enjoyed by other privileged communities. While all are enjoying the fruits of freedom, the Nepalis who fought for India's freedom and sacrificed and suffered most during freedom movement are deprived of the fruits of it. The Nepalis are one of the educationally, economically and socially most disadvantaged communities of Assam and yet their demand for S.T. is not yet fulfilled. Memoramdums submitted to the Government and representations made before the Backward Class Commission on behalf of the Nepalis are denied and kept unattended. The voice of Nepalis is drowned in the louder demand of the other communities like Tai Ahom, Koch Rajbangsi, Moran Matak etc.. For the Tea-tribes of Assam 100 new High schools are proposed to be established in tea garden areas and more seats to be reserved in the Medical and Engg. Colleges. But not a single seat has been reserved for the Nepali students who passed out from Assamese medium schools. Practically, nothing is envisaged for the Nepali community of Assam who are more backward educationally, socially and economically than other tribes instead, the benefit of protection.

In order to protect the interest of the tribal population of Assam, in 1946 the Government of Assam constituted 33 number of blocks called Tribal

Belts in seven districts of Assam comprising 5713 square miles area. This provision was made under Section 160 of Assam Land and Revenue Regulation. These areas were reserved for the indigenous tribal population of the following categories—(1) Plain tribals, (2) Hill Tribals, (3) Tea garden Tribals, (4) Santhals, and (5) Nepali cultivators/graziers. The Nepalis living within the Tribal Belts were given the status of "Protected Class" together with the Tribal people. The Nepalis were happy. But this benefit given for Nepalis was withdrawn by the Government of Assam in 1969 by a Notification No.RSD 26-64 PI/15 dated 27-6-1969 issued by the Secretary, Government of Assam, Revenue (Settlement) Department for reasons best known to them.

There was Government apathy and discriminatory treatment towards the Nepali flood victims. Large areas of Grazing Reserves were de-reserved and distributed to cultivators who lost their lands due to flood erosion but Nepalis were denied this benefit. Instead the Nepali graziers were evicted from the grazing reserves in order to rehabilitate the local flood victims. A few examples are given below.

In the Mangaldoi sub-division under Shekhar Mouza, about 18/20 Nepali families were evicted from villages named Volayatar and Nanke Samara in 1970. These Nepali families were flood affected cultivators who came from village Singri after they became the victims of Brahmaputra flood[2], whereas other flood affected families belonging to non-Nepalis communities were allowed to settle down in those villages.

Another 336 Nepali families were evicted from villages Kachuil, Gumbasti, Phulbari, Kalajhar etc. under the Mouza Udalguri. These families were also flood affected and 43 families were ex-servicemen families.[3] Here also only the Nepalis families were evicted.

Another 705 Nepali families who were victims of land erosion due to Brahmaputra flood in Lakhimpur district who possessed certificate to that effect from the APO, Chapakhowa, were mercilessly evicted from No.15, Chungajan forest reserve under district Sibsagar, while other flood affected people living side by side were not touched at all.[4]

Forty-five thousand bighas of land was de-reserved from Amteka forest reserve under Kokrajhar Sub-Division for settlement to landless flood affected farmers in 1970. This resulted in eviction of many Nepali Khuties who had to shift their cattle sheds. There were some flood affected Nepali households also among those who applied for settlement of land. The Sub-Divisional Officer, Kokrajhar prepared a list of some thousands of beneficiaries but not a single Nepali family's name included. A delegation which included Shri Uttam Chandra Brahma, local MLA and Shri Bishnulal Upadhyaya MLA met the Chief Minister, Assam on 5-12-70 who instructed the concerned officer to consider the cases of all deserving farmers without discrimination.[5]

Nepali graziers who were keeping their Khuties in the Grazing Reserves at Lawkhowa, Aradonga, Amteka etc. ever since fifty years were evicted for which the graziers were greatly hard hit. On 15-11-70 the representatives of Assam Gorkha Sammelan met the Chief Minister, Forest Minister of Assam and Shri Vijay Chandra Bhagawati, the President of the Assam Pradesh Congress Committee and apprised them of the problems faced by the milk producers of the state[6], but to no avail.

Problems of Backward Class, ST and SC

The Article 46 of the Directive Principles of State Policy of the constitution of India enjoins the state Governments to promote the educational and economic interests of the weaker sections of the people, particularly of the Scheduled Castes and the backward tribes, and to protect them from social injustice and all forms of exploitations. In order to comply with the above directives under Article 46 there was the need to investigate into the conditions of socially and educationally backward people within the territory of India and to identify those communities who need to be assisted and to prescribe the nature and quantity of grants to be given to them. For this purpose, the President of India constituted, under Article 340 of the Constitution, the first Backward Class Commission on the 29 January, 1953, under the Chairmanship of Kaka Kalelkar. It was also known as the first Backward Class Commission or Kaka Kalelkar Commission. The references of the Commission laid down in the Government Notification were:

1. To determine the criteria to be adopted in considering whether any sections of the people in the territory of India, in respect of the SC and ST as socially and educationally backward classes, using such criteria it was to prepare a list of such classes setting out also their approximate members and their territorial distribution.

2. To investigate the conditions of all such socially and educationally backward classes, and to determine under which they labour and make recommendation.
   (a) As to the steps that should be taken by the Union or any state to remove such difficulties or to improve their economic condition,
   (b) As to the grants that should be made for the purpose by the Union or state and the conditions subject to which such grants should be made.
   (c) To investigate such other matters as the President may hereafter refer to them, and
   (d) To present to the President a report setting out the facts as found by them and making such recommendations as they think proper.

For identifying socially and educationally backward classes, the Commission adopted the following criteria:

1. Low social position in the traditional caste hierarchy of Hindu society.
2. Lack of general educational advancement among the major section of a caste or community.
3. Inadequate or no representation in the Government services.
4. Inadequate representation in the field of trade, commerce and industry.

The Commission visited various places inhabited by socially and educationally disadvantaged communities, met their delegations and accepted memorandums. The Commission came to Assam, during its course of investigation when the Nepali leaders of Assam also submitted memorandum to the Commission. The Commission, after detailed enquiry and careful examination, submitted its report to Government on 30

March, 1955 which contained a list of 2399 backward classes or communities for the entire country, of which 837 had been classified as the most backward. Some of the salient features of the recommendation were as follows:

1. There should be caste-wise enumeration of population during decadal census.
2. There should be 70 per cent reservation of seats in all technical and professional institutions for students of backward classes.
3. Special economic measures should be taken to uplift the OBCs economically through such programmes as extensive land reforms, recognition of village economy, *Bhoodan* movement, development of livestock, dairy farming, cattle insurance, bee-keeping, piggery, fisheries.
4. Minimum reservation of vacancies in all government services and local bodies for other backward classes should be on the following scale: for class I–25 per cent, for class II–33.5 per cent, for class III and IV—40 per cent.

The lists of the castes and communities, recognised as backward class and other backward classes were, however, published by instalments after scrutiny at the state Government levels. After much delay the list of Nepali castes recognised as backward class came out in 1975 under Government Notification No. TAD/BC/268/75/37 dated 20th November, 1975, which mentioned—Thapa, Gurung, Lama, Magar, Newar, Lohar, Damai, Gaine, Rai, Chhetri, Limbu, Sarki, i.e. Cobbler (Vide Government Notification at Appendix V, attached).

This report of Kaka Kalelkar was, however, not implemented by the Government of India on the ground that it did not apply any objective tests for identifying the backward class. Thus, there was the need of a Second Backward Class Commission.

On 1st January, 1979, the Second Backward Class Commission was constituted by the Government of India under the Chairmanship of B.P. Mondal. It was the Janata Government under the Prime Minister Morarji Desai. The Commission after completion of its investigation, submitted its report in December, 1980. In its report, the Commission estimated that 52 per cent of the total population of the country (excluding SC and ST), belonged to 3,743 different castes and communities, who were socially and educationally backward. The number of backward class in central list of OBC has now increased to 5013 in 2006 as per National Commission for Backward Class. Mondal Commission recommended 27 per cent reservation for the OBC and 22.5 per cent reservation for the SC and ST and the rest for generals.

By that time Janata Government had been replaced by Congress Government and Prime Minister, Indira Gandhi was not interested to implement the recommendation of Mondal Commission, as it had become a contentious issue in the political corridor. After being relegated to ten years, the V.P. Singh Government accepted the report of the Mondal Commission on 7 August, 1990. Mondal Commission had recommended 27 per cent reservation for the OBC and 22.5 per cent reservation for the SC and ST and the rest 49.5 per cent for others. Hardly had the Government started implementation of the Report, a section of disgruntled people filed a petition in the Supreme Court challenging the constitutional validity of the Mondal Commission report, and the Supreme Court in its turn stayed the operation until final hearing. On 16 November, 1992, the SC upheld the Government order, with the opinion that the caste was an acceptable indicator of backwardness in India. Other backward class (OBC) is a collective term used by Government to classify castes which are socially and educationally disadvantaged.

Thus, the recommendation of the Mondal Commission was finally implemented from 1992. With a view to see that the genuine and deserving people may not be deprived of the benefit and the high income group and influential people do not take the upper hand, the Government of India put up a bar on the creamy layer class of people whose income is Rs.1 lakh or more in 1993, which was subsequently increased to Rs. 2.5 lakh in 2004, Rs. 4.5 in 2008 and to Rs. 6 lakh in 2013.

The list of twelve Nepali communities notified as backward classes by the Government of Assam in 1960 is still applicable although its implementation was put on hold until 1975. But the list of communities recognised by Government was not acceptable to the Nepali community for three reasons: firstly, the Lohar (Blacksmith), Damai (Tailor), Gaine (Panegyrist) and Sarki (Cobbler) mentioned in the list who are socially disadvantaged among Nepali society were not recognised as Scheduled Castes by Government. When the professionally low caste communities of other Hindu societies are recognised as Scheduled Caste, the Nepali professional castes belonging to the same low castes also should have been given the status of Scheduled Caste category instead of putting them in backward class. Secondly, the Nepali Brahmins, though belong to higher social rank, are educationally more backward than the Brahmins of other Indian communities in India. The criteria for identifying backward class, as accepted by Backward Class Commission, being either educationally or socially disadvantaged group, the Nepali Brahmins certainly fulfil one of the two criteria, i.e. educationally backward and hence they should have been included among the backward class. And lastly, the list of Nepali backward class is not exhaustive as there are still other Tibeto-Mongolian communities called Sherpa, Yolmo, Sonowal, Lepcha, Chepang etc.who are equally or more backward than those already recognised as Backward by the

Government. Therefore they deserve to be included together with other backward communities. Because of all these reasons, the Assam Gorkha Sammelan had submitted a memorandum to the Government of India on 24 July, 1968 to review and reconsider the case of the backward Nepalis of Assam. The All Assam Nepali Students Association was also concerned for this discrimination and submitted a memorandum to the Prime Minister of India on 24 July, 1980. In their memorandum, they pleaded for inclusion of Damai, Kami, Gaine, Bhujel, and Sarki, who are low caste Hindus, in the SC list and Rai, Limbu, Magar, Gurung, Bhutia, Lepcha etc. in the ST list. As regards upper caste Brahmins of Nepali community, they were equally backward educationally and economically and hence, the Assam Gorkha Sammelan adopted a resolution demanding inclusion of them in the OBC list in its 18th Annual Conference held at Margherita (Dibrugarh) on December 30, 1984.The principles of natural justice demand that simply because a person is born in Brahmin caste, one should not be denied the right to education and other benefits. According to Mondal Commission report, more than half (52%) of the India's population are socially and educationally disadvantaged and by that standard, one hundred per cent of the Nepalis in Assam belong to this socially and educationally disadvantaged group.

West Bengal and Sikkim Recognised as ST

It may be mentioned that the West Bengal Government has recognised some of the Tibeto-Mongoloid groups of Nepali community as the Scheduled Tribes who are considered as backward class in Assam. The Sikkim Government also has recognised the Limbu and Tamang communities as Scheduled Tribe but in Assam they are simply backward class. This difference of categorisation of the same group of castes and communities in different states surely points out to the fact of clear deviation from the principles and criteria laid down by the Backward Commission. This should not have happened under the same Ministry of Social Justice and Empowerment and the supervision of the same National Commission for Backward Classes. These discrepancies have occasioned with great discrimination and injustice to a section of the same group of people living in Assam. These disgruntled people belonging to Tamang and Limbu communities have been requesting the Government of Assam to restore them to their legitimate right to be recognised as ST since several years but the government is putting a deaf ear. The Purbanchal Tamang Buddhist Sangha has been clamouring for inclusion Tamang (Lama) group of Buddhist people in the ST category since more than ten years. This Tamang (Lama) and Limbu communities have been included in the ST category by the West Bengal and Sikkim Governments but in Assam they are clubbed with backward class. The other Tibeto-Burman linguistic communities like Rai, Limbu, Gurung, Magar, Newar etc. also equally deserve to be recognised as ST. In a significant positive move, the Ministry of Tribal Affairs, Government of India, by a Notification No. 12016/6/2001-C&LM-I(Pt.) dated 22nd April, 2016, constituted a committee to examine and recommend the granting of ST status to eleven Gorkha communities, *viz.*—Newar, Gurung, Magar, Rai, Bhujel, Khas, Sunuwar, Yakkha, Dhimal, Thami and Jogi, living in Sikkim and other Gorkha dominated states. The Committee was headed by Ashok Pai, Joint Secretary, Ministry of Tribal Affairs, Government of India. Unfortunately, the matter remained there only without being further processed and followed up.

During recent years the Tai Ahom, Koch Rajbansi, Chutia, Moran, Motak, and Tea Tribes are also trying to get recognition as Scheduled Tribes and it is learnt that the Government of Assam has recommended their cases and sent for approval of the Ministry of Social Justice and Empowerment, New Delhi. The All Assam Adhivasi Students Association has called for removal of the 'area restriction' provision to pave the way for inclusion of sixty lakhs strong Tea Adhibasi population of the state in the Scheduled Tribe (ST) list. The Adhivasis in states like Bihar, Chhattisgarh, Jharkhand, Madhya Pradesh, Orissa, West Bengal and Tripura are recognised as STs, by their respective state governments, but they come under OBC in Assam. Demanding recognition as ST, the All Assam Adhivasi Students Association staged a demonstration outside the D.C. Office in Tinsukia on the 15th December, 2017.[7] They deserve it and should get it, but Nepalis should not be denied their legitimate demand, for they deserve more than the above mentioned six groups of Assam's indigenous communities. The demand of the Nepalis living in Assam for generations is still lying un-noticed and un-fulfilled for more than half a century. Recently, out of the above six communities of Assam only three *viz.*, Koch Rajbansi, Chutia and Moran have been included as ST by Government of Assam, but by doing that none of the group of six communities are happy and satisfied as revealed them.

Reservation of Seats for Backward Class

After much delay the Government of Assam issued a Notification No. ABP.131/84/18 dated 20-6-84 which allowed reservation of seats for students belonging to SC/ST and other Backward Class in Technical, Medical etc. institutions under Education, Medical, Veterinary, Health, etc. departments at the same percentage at which vacancies are reserved for them in appointments to public services. The Notification also mentioned the percentage of reservation allowed to SC/ST/Other Backward Class categories under the Assam ST/SC (Reservation of vacancies in Service and Posts) Act, 1978 and under the Personnel Department

O.M. No. ABP. 338/83/14, dated 4-1-84, In the notification Reservation in favour of SC and ST and Other Backward Classes were mentioned as follows:

Members of the SC Class	7%
Members of the ST Class	10%
Members of the OBC Class	5%
Members of More OBC	15%

(The Notification mentioned above is enclosed at Appendix IV)

Unfortunately, the Notification mentioned above remained in paper only in respect of the Nepali Backward Class candidates, as no one got admission so far in any of the notified departmental institutions.

Question of Indian Citizenship

It was often observed that the Assam Government bureaucrats were, by and large, overenthusiastic to enforce the rules and laws of the country without properly knowing them and by doing that, they caused untold harassment and injustice to the common citizens, especially the Nepalis. Despite the fact of clarifications made by the Government of Assam from time to time about the citizenship and voting rights of the Nepalis living in Assam for generations, the concerned officers had been found to commit the same mistake again and again. In 1960 during the time of revision of electoral rolls for the third general election in Assam, the Block Development Officer of Bokakhat Development Block issued notice No. GB/BPG/2/21/71/128 dated 21-11-60 to all concerned, stating that in accordance with the instruction given by the Sub-Divisional Officer (Civil) in order to prove whether the Nepalis living in India are actually Indians or not, they have to show reliable documents like, Citizenship Certificate or certificates from the Mouzadar, Gaon Bura or prominent person of the village and to prove their permanent residence.

This matter, having been brought to the notice of MLA Bishnulal Upadhyaya by the affected Nepalis of Bokakhat Development Block, a Starred Assembly Question No. 688 was placed in the Assembly by the MLA. The following were the questions and the replies given by the Chief Minister of Assam, Shri Mahendra Mohan Choudhury.

Assembly Question No. 688 asked by Shri Bishnulal Upadhyaya MLA and the Reply of Assam Chief Minister, Shri Mahendra Mohan Choudhury.

Question: Will the Chief Minister be pleased to state—

(a) Whether a memorandum was submitted to him by the questioner on 25 March, 1971 demanding a thorough enquiry regarding deletion of the names of about 4500 bonafide Nepali voters from the electoral roll of 1970 under Dibrugarh Parliamentary Constituency specially in Sadiya, Chapakhowa, Chunpura, Jonai and Dhola area?

Ans: (a) Yeas, but according to information available with government it is not a fact that the number of Nepalis voters who are bonafide citizens of India under Article 5 of the constitution of India have been deleted from the electoral rolls.

Question (e) Whether it is a fact that those voters were debarred from voting under Section 22 and 23 of the Representation of Peoples Act, 1950?

Ans (e) Yes, the deletions were made under Section 22 of the Representation of Peoples Act, 1950 in the case of those non-eligible persons who have not acquired the citizenship of India under Article 5 of the Constitution and who were to acquire this right of naturalisation under Section 6(1) of the Citizenship Act, 1955. The deletion of names were made after proper verification.

But Section 23 of the Act deals with inclusion of names of eligible voters.

It appeared that the question of deletion of names from electoral rolls of Nepalis who were not Indian citizens under Article 5 of the constitution, arose from the order dated 17 May, 1960 issued by Shri A.B.Dasgupta, Chief Electoral Officer, Assam instructing all Deputy Commissioners and Sub-Divisional Officers (Elections) to determine the national status of Nepali settlers in Assam for the purpose of inclusion of their names in the electoral rolls. The instruction was as follows:

> I am directed to state that the views of the Central Government are that the Nepalis who cannot claim Indian citizenship under Article 5 of the constitution cannot automatically become Indian citizens merely by long and continuous residence in India. These Nepalis have to acquire Indian citizenship first under the relevant section of the electoral rolls of the constituency in which they are residing.
>
> Further, a person who is not a citizen of the country specified in the first schedule to the Citizenship Act, 1955 can acquire Indian citizenship by naturalisation under Section 6(i) of the Act. As such Nepalese who fall within the category of persons stated above, may be advised to apply for naturalisation of Indian citizenship under Section 6(i) of the said Act subject to their satisfying the conditions mentioned in the third schedule to the Act.
>
> I am accordingly to request you to bring this to the notice of Election Registration Officers so that the anomalies in the preparation of the rolls may be avoided. Unless the Electoral Registration Officer is satisfied that the Nepalis are covered by Article 5 of

> the constitution or have acquired Indian Citizenship as indicated above, their names should not be included in the electoral rolls.

So, the above order of the Chief Electoral Officer of Assam is clear enough: that all Nepalis are not to produce citizenship certificate, because those Nepalis who are "covered by Article 5 of the constitution, and those who have acquired Indian citizenship" are automatically the citizens of India.

Yet another Electoral jeopardy

In 1971, a mid-term election to the Lok Sabha seat for Dibrugarh constituency was conducted by the Government. On the stipulated date of poll people went to exercise their right of franchise to their respective polling stations. As before the Nepali voters also went and joined the bee-line to the polling booths. Reaching the Presiding officer they were utterly dismayed to find that their names were struck out with red-ink without their knowledge or without notifying them about the reason of doing so and giving them the opportunity to defend their cases. They were refused to cast their votes. The names of all Nepali voters irrespective of citizenship right were reddened with ink. They returned home deeply anguished and disillusioned. For there could be no reason whatsoever for such an act of wholesale disenfranchisement of the legitimate voters who had cast their votes several times in the past. This matter having been brought to the notice of the Dibrugarh District branch of the Assam Gorkha Sammelan, on the 25th March, 1971. Shri Bishnulal Upadhyaya, MLA, tabled an Assembly Question No. 688 asking the Chief Minister of Assam to conduct a thorough enquiry about the matter. The details of the Assembly Question and Answer is given below:

Q. 688. Will the Chief Minister be pleased to state—

(a) Whether a memorandum was submitted to him by the questioner demanding a thorough enquiry regarding deletion of the names of about 4500 bona fide Nepali voters from the electoral rolls of 1970 under Dibrugarh Parliamentary Constituency especially in Sadiya, Chapkhowa, Chunpara, Jonai and Dhola area?

Shri Mahendra Mohan Choudhury, Chief Minister replied:

A. (a) Yes, but according to information available with Government, it is not a fact that the names of Nepali voters who were bona fide citizens of India under Article 5 of the constitution of India, have been deleted from the electoral rolls.

Q. (b) Whether it is a fact that those voters were debarred from voting under section 22 and 23 of the Representation of Peoples Act, 1950?

A. (b) Yes, the deletions were made under Section 22 of the Representation of Peoples Act, 1950 in the case of those non-eligible persons who have not acquired the citizenship of India under Article 5 of the Constitution and who were to acquire this right by naturalisation under Section 6(1) of the Citizenship Act, 1955. The deletions were made after proper verification. But Section 23 of the Act deals with inclusion of names of eligible voters.

Q.(c) Whether the government is aware of the feeling and sentiment of the bona fide Nepalese who have made Assam their motherland?

A.(c) Yes, Government have no intention to debar such Nepalis who acquired Indian citizenship under the provisions of the Indian Citizenship Act, 1955.

Q. (d) Whether it is a fact that the questioner has also submitted similar memorandum to the Special Secretary,

Appointment and Election Department and the Chief Electoral Officer on 24th March, 1971?

A. (d) Yeas.

Q.(e) Whether it is a fact that the Chief Minister on receipt of the allegations was pleased to assure the questioner that he would enquire into the matter deputing a special Commission to Dibrugarh and take action against the officer responsible? Whether any enquiry has been made, and if so what is the report?

A. (e) The matter is being enquired into.

A delegation was also led by Shri Bishnulal Upadhyaya MLA which met Shri Mahendra Mohan Choudhury, Chief Minister of Assam and urged upon him to cause immediate enquiry into it and to correct the voter list. The matter, however, remained unattended under the red-tape until the time for Revision of Voter List for the next general election came up. Shri Bishnulal Upadhyaya MLA reminded the Chief Secretary, Government of Assam to inform him about the action taken by the 3rd June, 1971.

In view of the delaying tactic of the Government, the Nepalis of Tinsukia in a meeting attended by all the Nepali voters of Dibrugarh district, adopted a resolution which decided to file a PIL Petition in the Supreme Court of India for dispensation of immediate justice. Knowing of this move by the Nepalis, Shri Bhavani Kumar Bhuyan, IAS, Special Secretary Election, Government of Assam visited Dibrugarh on the 9th August, 1971 for enquiry, when he was handed over a copy of the memorandum of the Nepali voters of Dibrugarh submitted to the Election Commission of India by Bal Bahadur Rai, President of the Dibrugarh District Committee. Thereafter, prompt action started by the Special Secretary, Assam who visited Dibrugarh, Chapakhowa, Tinsukia, Sadiya etc. and met all the concerned D.Cs, S.D.Os, Assistant Political Officers and District Returning

Officers and gave them detailed instructions for revision of electoral rolls.

Accordingly Revised Voter Lists were prepared in which the 3500 deleted names of Nepali voters were included. This fact of inclusion of 3500 names of Nepali voters in the revised electoral rolls go to prove that the allegation made by the Nepalis of Dibrugarh about the deletion of their names was true and that the statement made by Shri Mahendra Mohan Choudhury, Chief Minister of Assam denying the accusation during his reply to the Assembly question mentioned above was not true. Bishnulal Upadhyaya, a true parliamentarian, quibbled—what was the basis of Chief Minister's reply? The fact of the matter was that, the Chief Minister was not at fault; he replied exactly as what was reported to him by his officers. It was the bureaucrat who committed the wrong and tried to cover up when the same was questioned. The bureaucrats were, more often than not, found to be over zealous in enforcing the law by presuming every Nepali to be a foreign national and every Muslim to be a Bangladeshi, and by doing that meted with a great injustice to the bona fide citizens of India. The aforesaid incident is only a tip of the ice-burg. There were thousands of innocent and simple Nepalis who were the citizens of India but had been debarred from exercising their right of franchise in various districts of Assam, that went unreported.

Question of Nepalese Citizenship in the Parliament

The issue of enrolment of names of the Nepalese in the electoral roll without verifying their citizenship status, at times, became so contentious that it was even dragged over to the floor of Indian Parliament by Shri Biswanarayan Shastri, MP (Lakhimpur) who raised a question in the Lok Sabha as follows:

3910. Shri Biswanarayan Shastri:

(a) Whether it is a fact that the Nepali citizens coming from Nepal and settled in India (Assam) have been registered as voters without having acquired Indian citizenship; and

(b) If so, the details thereof?

Shri Jagannath Rao, Minister of State, Ministry of Law and Social Welfare, Government of India, replied as follows:

A. (a) and (b) The information is being collected from the Chief Electoral Officer, Assam.

After the reply had been received from the Chief Electoral Officer, Assam, it was tabled before the Parliament on the 18th December, 1970. The reply ran as follows:

> (a) and (b) "The Chief Electoral Officer, Assam has reported that it is not possible to ascertain whether any Nepali citizen settled down in Assam has been registered as an elector in any Assembly constituency in the state without having acquired Indian citizenship. The Electoral Registration Officers who are asked to conduct enquiries in the matter have reported that the electoral rolls do not contain information regarding the community to which a particular elector belongs. Consequently, it is not possible for the Electoral Registration Officer to locate the entries relating to Indian citizens of Nepali origin without conducting a thorough enquiry on the spot in respect of each and every entry in the electoral rolls of the state. The work will require a very large staff and involve a considerable expenditure, besides an enquiry of this nature would arouse legitimate fear in the minds of large number of Indian Nepalis

> who are genuine citizens of India and whose names are already registered in the electoral roll, that their names would be deleted. The Chief Electoral Officer, Assam, placed these difficulties and apprehensions before the Chief Election Commissioner. The Chief Election Commissioner, therefore, decided that no such enquiry need be conducted as it would not be possible for the electoral machinery in the state to do this work with any degree of accuracy."

The report mentioned above, as submitted by the Chief Electoral Officer, Assam explained the actual difficulties experienced by the working staff on the ground. It was practically not possible on the part of the Electoral Registration officers to identify each and every voter in the Electoral roll to be a Nepali who came from Nepal and to institute an enquiry as to whether he is a citizen of India and to decide whether to include or delete his name from the electoral roll. The Election Commission of India after careful examination of the problem explained by the Chief Electoral Officer agreed with him and decided that "no such enquiry need be conducted as it would not be possible for the election machinery in the state to do this work with any degree of accuracy.

In this context, the General Secretary, Dibrugarh District Committee of the Assam Gorkha Sammelan also received a letter No. 287/AS/1/70(EBV)40919 dated 11th December, 1970 from the Under Secretary, Election Commission of India, New Delhi in reply to his memorandum No.DDGS/CI/1-70 dated 24 November, 1970. The letter, among other things, mentioned as follows:

> "...The Commission also felt that an enquiry of this nature would arouse legitimate fear in the minds of

> large number of Indian citizens of Nepalis origin who are already registered in the electoral rolls that their names would be deleted from them. In the circumstances it was decided that no such enquiry need be conducted. It may be stated, it is not the province of the Election Commission to conduct enquiries as to the citizenship of persons of any foreign country, domiciled or resident in India and that this task appropriately belongs to those who are charged with duty of registering foreigners as Indian citizen."

Finally, the Election Commission of India issued its final decision on 7th July, 1978 on the issue of citizenship of Nepalis/ Gorkhas, which is given below:

Decision of Election Commission of India

Finally, on 7 July, 1978, Mr. V. Naga Subramaniam, Secretary to the Election Commission of India issued instructions to the Chief Electoral Officers of Uttar Pradesh, Bihar, West Bengal, Assam, Manipur, Meghalaya, Nagaland, Arunachal Pradesh and Mizoram regarding the electoral rolls registration of Nepalis origin as below[8]:

> For the past several years, the Commission has been seized with the problem of registration of persons of Nepali origin in our electoral rolls. On the one hand, there were allegations that Nepalis who are not Indian citizens have been registered in the electoral rolls in large numbers and on the other hand, there were complaints that the names of Nepalis who became Indian citizens by long residence and had been registered in the electoral rolls, were removed

> from such rolls for want of proof of their Indian citizenship.
>
> After careful consideration, the commission in August 1971 issued instructions that in the case of persons of Nepali origin who have already been registered in the electoral rolls, the wives and children should also be included. As regards other persons of Nepali origin settled in India, it is a question of fact whether they are citizens of India under the provisions of Article 5 of the constitution, or under Section 3 and 4 of the Citizenship Act, and it should be decided after due enquiry.

It may be mentioned that the Government of India also clarified misconception, in this regard besides the laws already in the place.The Ministry of Home Affairs, Government of India, New Delhi, in a Gazette Notification dated 23rd August, 1988, further clarified the misconception, if any, regarding the citizenship right of the Gorkhas living in India. Copy of the said Gazette Notification is reproduced below:

Citizenship Issue of Gorkhas

Gazette Notification published in Gazette of India, Extra-ordinary, Part-I, Section-I, dated 23rd August, 1988. No. 26011/6/88-ICI. Government of India, Ministry of Home Affairs, New Delhi the 23rd August, 1988.

Notification

Whereas it has come to the notice of the Central Government that there have been some misconception about the citizenship at the commencement of the constitution of India of certain class of persons commonly known as Gorkhas who had settled in India at such commencement.

And whereas it is considered necessary to clear such misconception. It is hereby clarified as follows:

1. As from the commencement of the constitution, that is, as from 26-1-1950 every Gorkha who had his domicile in the territory of India, as defined in Article 1(2) of the constitution of India, and
   (a) Who was born in the territory of India, or
   (b) Either of whose parents was born in the territory of India,
   (c) Who had been ordinarily resident in the territory of India for not less than five years before such commencement, shall be a citizen of India as provided in Article 5 of the constitution of India.
2. No such person as is referred to in the paragraph (1) above shall be a citizen of India or be deemed to be a citizen of India if he has voluntarily acquired the citizenship of any foreign state as provided in Article 9 of the constitution of India.
3. Every person who is citizen of India at the commencement of the constitution as aforesaid shall continue to be such a citizen subject to the provision of any law that may be made by Parliament as provided in Article 10 of such constitution of India.
4. The provision of the Citizenship Act, 1955 and the rules and orders made thereunder shall apply to the persons referred to in paragraph (1) after the commencement of the constitution. (See Appendix No.)

S/D

(Indra Misra)

Joint Secretary to the Government of India

Ministry of Home Affairs, New Delhi

From the above decision of the Election Commission of India and further clarification by the Government of India, Ministry of Home Affairs, *vis-à-vis* the provisions of the constitution of India and the Citizenship Act, 1955 we find that the Nepalis/Gorkhas living in India will fall under the following three categories.

1. Citizens of India

(a) Those, who are domicile in India at the commencement of constitution, i.e., 26-1-1950. (Under Article 5 of constitution)
(b) Those, who are born in India. (Under Sec. 3 of Citizenship Act, 1955)
(c) Those, either of whose parents was born in India. (Under Sec. 4 of Citizenship Act, 1955)
(d) The wives of the citizens of India.

The above mentioned category of Nepalis/Gorkhas become automatically citizens of India and eligible for all the civil and political rights including right to franchise on attainment of 18 years age.

2. Domicile in Assam

Nepalis/Gorkhas who enter India after 26-1-1950 or/and do not fulfil the conditions stated at 1 above can become a domicile in Assam under Rule 307(2) of Assam Executive Manual which reads as follows:

> "A person who is not a native of Assam shall be deemed to be domicile in Assam only when he becomes the owner of homestead (House and land) in the province and has already lived for ten years and intends to live there until he dies."

The children of such persons are also deemed to be domicile.

A domiciled person can be legally considered as "Permanent Resident". When the above conditions are fulfilled the Deputy Commissioner is authorised to give a certificate of domicile.

3. Foreign National

Those who come to India after 26-1-1950 and do not fulfil any of the above condition cannot claim Indian citizenship merely by domicile in India, nor can they be eligible to cast vote. They can, however, apply for naturalisation under Sec. 6 of the Citizenship Act, 1955 and become Indian citizen. They can stay in India, possess any property and carry on any trade or business by virtue of Article 7 of the Indo-Nepal Treaty of Peace and Friendship, 1950, provided there is no restriction in entry into any part of India by any special Order promulgated by the Government of India. It may be mentioned here that the Government of India, Ministry of Home Affairs, New Delhi has by its Notificatin No. 25022/110/76-FI(11) dated 30th July, 1976 imposed restriction on Nepalese nationals to enter into the North Eastern Region with immediate effect under Foreigners (Restricted Area) Orders 1963 (Amendment Order, 1976). Hence, despite the Indo-Nepal Treaty of Peace and Friendship, 1950 or any other agreement or law in place, no Nepali national can enter North East region with effect from 30 July, 1976 without valid permit from the proper authority.

Citizenship Question Raked Up Again

Despite the expressed provisions of the constitution of India and the Indian Citizenship Act, 1955 in place, and also the Notification of the Government of India, Ministry of Home Affairs, dated 23rd August, 1988 clarifying the misconceptions lingering about the Indian citizenship of the Gorkhas/Nepalis living in India, the Deputy Commissioner/Sub-Divisional

Officers, Mangaldoi once again raked up the question of Nepalis Indian citizenship by issuing indiscriminate Notices to all Nepalis living in the district to prove their citizenship in India on the stipulated dates and places. Notices were issued even to such persons like Dr. Madhav Upadhyaya, grandson of Chhabilal Upadhyaya, the veteran freedom fighter of India. Such uncalled for and politically motivated act of the district authorities brought about a state of mass fear psychosis among the simple and peaceful Nepalis. The Assam Gorkha Sammelan held an emergent meeting on the 14 June, 1979 at Maradhansiri (Rauta) with Bishnulal Upadhyaya, MLA in the chair and decided to take a delegation to the Chief Minister of Assam, Golap Borbora and to the Chief Electoral Officer of Assam. The meeting selected the following persons to form the delegation:

1. Bishnulal Upadhyaya, MLA, Behali
2. Padam Bahadur Chauhan, MLA, Nagrijuli
3. Cilvious Kandupan, BL, Mangaldoi
4. Kul Bahadur Chhetri, Margherita
5. Jay Narayan Luitel, MA, Tezpur
6. Tarapati Upadhyaya, MABT, Odalguri
7. Bhavani Prasad Upadhyaya, Tezpur
8. Durga Prasad Upadhyaya, MA, Tezpur
9. Chandra Mohan Chhetri, Odalguri
10. Kewal Praad Sharma, Rauta
11. Shisir Kumar Gurung, Maligaon
12. Ganesh Bahadur Chhetri, Suklai
13. Tarabir Chhetri, Teliagaon
14. Khemraj Adhikari, MA, LLB, Tezpur
15. Rewati Upadhyaya, B.Sc., Rauta
16. Pahal Thapa, MA, Kaliabar
17. Hari Gajural, MA, Biswanath
18. Krishna Chhetri, MA, LLB, Gauhati
19. Jhandi Upadhyaya, MA, Tezpur

20. Amarnath Upadhyaya, BA, Tezpur
21. Nar Bahadur Chhetri, BA, Tangla
22. Ramesh Chandra Saharia, MLA, Tangla
23. Nagen Sharma, MLA, Kalaigaon.

Accordingly, the delegation called on the Chief Minister of Assam and the Chief Electoral Officer at Dispur, who were, during that time, under so much political pressure that they could not give out their opinion for fear of agitation by political forces. It was the time of the beginning of Assam movement in the wake of foreigners issue spearheaded by All Assam Students Union (AASU) and All Assam Ganasangram Parishad (AAGP) which included Assam Yubak Samaj, Lawyers Association and Asam Sahitya Sabha. It would be pertinent here to discuss, at some length, about the situation prevalent in Assam in that time.

We may recall that the infamous Assam movement started from Mangaldoi in 1979 when the issue of foreign national cropped up among the Assamese people because of the alarming statement made by S.L. Shakdhar, the Chief Election Commissioner on the 24th October, 1978. Shakdhar said:

> "I would like to refer to the alarming situation in some states, especially in the North Eastern region, wherefrom reports are coming regarding large-scale inclusions of foreign nationals in the electoral rolls. In one case, the population in 1971 census recorded an increase as high as 34.98 per cent over 1961 census figures, and this increase was attributed to the influx of a large number of persons from foreign countries. The influx has become a regular feature."[9]

The student leaders of Assam took the above pronouncement of S.L. Shakdhar, Chief Election Commissioner seriously as a timely warning for them to act upon. Coincidently, the

Mangaldoi Parliamentary seat fell vacant on 28 March, 1979 due to the death of Hiralal Patwari, the Janata MP and preparation for holding bye-election to fill up the vacancy started. As the revision of electoral rolls began some 70,000 complaints were filed challenging the citizenship of a large number of persons of whom mostly were the Bangladeshis and Nepalis who had already exercised their right of franchise in earlier elections. The student's Union also successfully held up the Bye-election of Mangaldoi constituency until the names of foreign nationals were removed from the electoral rolls. Actually, the student leaders magnified the Mangaldoi issue which generated a very strong fear-psychosis among a large section of Assamese middle class people. It was alleged that a large number of fabricated complaints were lodged even by using the state police machinery with tacit support of the government. According to Dinesh Goswami, leader of the Assam Gana Parishad, 10,000 complaint forms supplied by Dispur election office not being sufficient another 40,000 forms were printed.[10]

Therefore, it was because of this situation that the Nepalis of Mangaldoi against whom complaints were filed by student leaders, were served with the Notices by the Deputy Commissioner/Sub-Divisional Officer to verify their Indian citizenship. The Chief Minister of Assam was well aware of this political conspiracy for which reason he could not reply frankly to MLAs (Bishnulal Updhyaya, Ramesh Saharia, Nagen Sarma etc.) who formed part of the delegation when they met him at Dispur. Having failed to get relief from the Chief Minister of Assam, the delegation decided to approach the Government of India for redressal of their grievance. Accordingly, on 11 July, 1979, a delegation consisting of nine members called on Shri M.M. Patel, Home Minister, Shri Santi Bhushan, Law Minister and Shri Atal Behari Bajpayee, Foreign Affair Minister of the

Janata Government at the Centre. They also met Smt. Indira Gandhi, President Congress(I) and also on different dates met Shri Dev Kanta Baruah, MP, Dr. Karan Singh, MP, Dinesh Goswami, MP, Tilak Gogoi, MP, Tarun Gogoi, MP, Lalit Kumar Daley, MP etc. The delegation apprised the Ministers and the MPs of the injustice meted out to the Nepalis living in Assam for generations who were genuine citizens of India. They also met S.L.Shakdhar, Chief Election Commissioner to whom they submitted some of their legal documents and authenticated before him about their citizenship rights in India.

1971—As the Cut-off Year

In compliance with the demand made by the student leaders of Assam for detection, deportation and deletion of the names of all foreign nationals from the electoral rolls, the Government of India passed the Illegal Migrants (Determination by Tribunals) Act, 1983. Under this Act, the Government agreed to detect and deport the foreign nationals who entered Assam after 25 March, 1971. This Act was actually meant for the illegal immigrants from Bangladeash after its coming into being as an independent country in 1971. But since the term "Foreign national" legally include the Nepalese nationals (a section of the Nepalis in Assam who are not the citizens of India) there arose a valid concern among the Nepalis that they might also be affected by the above Act. The Assam Gorkha Sammelan immediately took up the matter with the Government of India requesting that the Nepalis who came to Assam after 25 March, 1971 should not be clubbed together with the Bangladeshis under the said Illegal Migrants (Determination by Tribunals) Act, 1983. Since the Nepalese nationals' entry into India and their privilege in the matter of residence, ownership of property and participation in trade or commerce have been vouchsafed by the Article 7 of the Indo-Nepal Treaty of Peace and Friendship, 1950 they should not be treated at par with other foreign nationals. The demand was logical and justified. The Nepali delegation consisted of Bishnulal Upadhyaya, MLA, Padam Bahadur Chauhan, MLA, Khemraj Adhikari and Binod Dahal who met Smt. Indira Gandhi, Prime Minister, Gyani Jailsingh, Home Minister, Pranab Kumar Mukherjee, Finance Minister and many others and submitted memorandum in this regard. The Illegal Migrants (Determination by Tribunals) Act, 1983 was, however, summarily rejected and dissociated with the Tribunal constituted under the Act, by the student leadership of Assam and, therefore, was not enforced at all. Later on the issues of detection and deportation of the Bangladeshis were dealt with according to the provisions of the Assam Accord executed between the Government of India and the student leadership in 1985.

Nepalis status after Assam Accord

The Assam Accord 1985 renders the legal status of the Nepalis living in Assam ambiguous and vulnerable. It clubs the Nepalis in the same category with Bangladeshis, and equates them with any one whom they brand as foreigner. The clause eight of the Assam Accord states that—"Foreigners who came to Assam on or after March 25, 1971 shall continue to be detected, deleted and expelled in accordance with law. Immediate and practical steps shall be taken to expel such foreigners". The Assam Accord completely disregards the standing bilateral treaties and agreements signed between Nepal and Government of India as regards the Indian Nepalis living in different states of India. In absence of any saving provision made in the Assam Accord in respect of Nepalis, according to Indo-Nepal Treaty, 1950, the Nepalis of Assam would be treated as foreigners subjected to be "detected in accordance with the provisions of the Foreigners Act,1946 and Foreigners (Tribunals) Order, 1964", as laid down under clause 3 of the Assam Accord. But the Nepalis living in Assam should be automatically protected by the Indo-Nepal Treaty of Peace and Friendship, 1950 and subsequent agreements from being tried, detected and expelled from any part of India. The Article 7 of the Indo-Nepal Treaty expressly "grants on reciprocal basis, to the nationals of one country in the territories of the other the same privileges in the matter of residence, ownership of property, participation in trade and commerce, movement and other privileges of a similar nature". So, the question of detection and expulsion of Nepalis from Assam does not arise at all. Of course, no Nepali has so far been expelled from Assam although some of them have been branded foreigners and subjected to trial in accordance with the provisions of the Foreigners Act, 1946 and Foreigners (Tribunals) Order, 1964.

Since 30 July, 1976, the State Governments of Assam and adjoining States were strictly vigilant on the nationals of Nepal not allowing them to enter into Assam as per Notification No.25022/110/76-F1(11) Government of India, Ministry of Home Affairs, New Delhi, dated 30 July, 1976 restricting Nepalese from entering North East under Foreigners (Restricted Areas) Orders, 1963 (Amended). The Secretary to the Government of Assam, Home (Political) Department in his letter No. 25022/110/76-F 1(1) dated 30-7-76 issued circulars to all the Deputy Commissioners and Sub-Divisional Officers of the Districts and Sub-Divisions instructing them to see that Nepalese nationals without RAP (Restricted Area Permit) are not allowed to enter or remain in Assam. The order of the Government of India directly infringes the Article 7 of the Indo-Nepal Treaty, 1950 as mentioned. Therefore, it is necessary that the matter should be reviewed between the two Governments of Nepal and India before it is acted upon. As the matter stands now, people from both the countries enter into one-another's country freely without passport or visa under the provisions of the above treaty. If the Indians are allowed to enter freely into any part of Nepal, it will be unfair to restrict the Nepalese from entering into the North Eastern part of India. Therefore, the restriction put against the Nepalese to enter into Assam by the Foreigners (Restricted Area) Orders 1963 amendment in 1976 is directly repugnant to the Indo-Nepal Treaty of Peace and Friendship, 1950. It is a fit case for Nepal Government to take up with the Government of India.

There are two categories of Nepalis living in India—the Nepalis permanently residing in India (1) who are the Indian nationals, permanently settled in Assam, and (2) the Nepalese nationals temporarily working in India who are not the citizens of India. The former are Indian citizens and enjoy all legal and constitutional rights as any other Indians do. They have fully integrated themselves with Indian national mainstream. They like to be identified as **Gorkhas/Indian Nepalis** in order to distinguish themselves from the later who are the **Nepalese citizens** living and earning in India under the provisions of the Article 7 of the Indo-Nepal treaty, 1950. But the local Indian people make no distinction between the two. They confuse and take the Indian Nepalis who are permanently settled in India to be newcomers from Nepal. More often than not, they brand them all as foreigners and harass them in various ways. They call them foreigners, delete their names from voter list and NRC and deprive them of their economic and political rights. It is tragic to say that despite all the contributions made by them, the Indian Nepalis living permanently in the North Eastern States are not treated kindly by their Indian counterparts.

The Ministry of Home Affairs, Government of India has, in its letter dated 24 September, 2018, addressed to Government of Assam, clarified about the constitutional position of the Indian Nepalis living in India.[11] The letter stated—"Members of the Gorkha community who were Indian citizens at the time of commencement of the Constitution, or those who are Indian citizens by birth, or those who have acquired Indian citizenship by registration or naturalisation in accordance with the provisions of the Citizenship Act, 1955, are **not foreigners** in terms of Section 2(a) of the Foreigners Act, 1946 as well as the Registration of Foreigners Act, 1939. **Therefore such cases will not be referred to the Foreigners Tribunals"**. It further emphasized that "any member of the Gorkha community holding Nepalese nationality who has arrived in India by land or air or the Nepal border even without a passport or visa and staying in India for any length of time, **shall not be treated as an illegal migrant** if he/she is in possession of any of the identity document, namely, the Nepalese passport, Nepalese citizenship certificate, voter identification card issued by the Election Commission of Nepal, limited validity Photo-identity certificate issued by Nepalese Mission in India when deemed necessary, and for children between age group of 10-18 years, photo ID is issued by the Principal of the school, if accompanied by parents having valid travel documents. No such document is required for children below the age group of 10 years, the communication added citing provisions of India-Nepal Treaty signed in 1950.

The above letter of the Ministry of Home Affairs, Government of India dated 24 September, 2018 is an important piece of document which makes the legal and political positions of the Nepalis living in India, crystal clear for future reference in respect of the Assam Accord, National Register of Citizenship (NRC), trial by Foreigners Tribunal or any other case that may arise concerning the constitutional status of the Nepalis living in India. Every Nepali/Gorkha in Assam must be well aware about his or her legal and constitutional positions as clarified by the Government of India by this document and/or if possible should possess a copy of the Government letter for future use, for the Government of Assam is going to implement the Clause 6 of the Assam Accord for which a High Level Committee under the Chairmanship of retired Judge, Biplab Kumar Sharma, has been constituted by Government of India on 15 July, 2019. A memorandum on behalf of the Nepalis in Assam has been submitted by a group of Nepali organisations on 21 August, 2019 together with many other memorandums by different organisations. We need to be well prepared in case of any injustice meted out to Gorkha community.

Clause Six of the Assam Accord

The Memorandum of understanding, popularly known Assam Accord was signed between the All Assam Students Union and the Government of India, Ministry of Home Affairs on the 15 August, 1985. The 6th Clause of the MOU was one of the salient features of the Assam Accord placed under the sub-head—Safeguards and economic development which stated as follows:

> Clause 6. Constitutional, legislative and administrative safeguards, as may be appropriate, shall be provided to protect, preserve and promote the cultural, social, linguistic identity and heritage of the Assamese people.

Here, the All Assam Students Union and many other intelligentsia of Assam interpreted the above expression "Assamese people" as Khilanjia Assamese people, in exclusion of other non-Assamese communities. This brought about a contentious question—who is a Khilanjia Assamese?

NOTES

1. Bishnulal Upadhyaya (1984). *Asame Nepaliharu*, Extended Edition, pp. xxxiv-xxxv.
2. Bulletin, No. 11, 12, *Assam Gorkha Sammelan*, p. 100.
3. *Ibid.*, p. 101.
4. *Ibid.*, p. 100.
5. *Ibid.*, p. 100.
6. *Ibid.*, p. 84.
7. *The Times of India*, English Daily, dated 16 December, 2017.
8. Election Commission of India, Niruachan Sadan, Ashoka Road, New Delhi, 7 July, 1978, No. 23-1-76.
9. M. Hussain (1993). *The Assam Movement*, p. 102.
10. *Ibid.*, p. 105.
11. *Shillong Times*, English Daily, dated 11-10-2018.

5

Conclusion

From the above discussion it has been crystal clear that there has been an integration of the Nepalis culture with Assamese society while keeping their own Nepali culture and tradition in tact. The Nepalis have adopted the language, customs and tradition of the Assamese society and at the same time preserved, protected and developed their own language, culture and tradition, in such a way as no other non-Assamese community living in Assam has done so far. Bishnulal Upadhyaya rightly said—"Nepalis have embraced Assam as their *Janmabhumi, Karmabhumi and Ramyabhumi*. The Nepalis of Assam have been striving hard to assimilate themselves with the larger Asamiya nationality, and have contributed decisively in giving the Asamiya language an absolute and dominant majority status in Assam. The Assamese people too found them to be simple, similar looking like themselves and welcomed the Nepalis with their open heart. They were largely well-accepted and well-treated in larger Assamese society. Jyoti Prasad Agarwala, a true patriot of Assam, in his poem "Axamiya Dekar Ukti" called the Nepalis of Assam as *Thaluwa Nepali*[1] which means an indigenous community of Assam.

Behind this integration of two socities there existed diplomatic mindset and hard work of Nepali leaders like Babu Chhabilal Upadhyaya, Bishnulal Upadhyaya, Bhakta Bahadur Pradhan and Dalbir Singh Lohar. They were pioneer leaders of Nepali people of Assam. From the very beginning they were inspired by Assamese leaders like Chandra Nath Sarma, Bijoy Chandra Bhagawati, Gahan Chandra Goswami, Bogiram Saikia etc. in the freedom movement of India. They led the Nepali people of Assam during freedom struggle. Babu Chhabilal Upadhyaya chaired the historic meeting held at Jorhat (Assam) on 17 April, 1921 in which a historic decision was taken to merge Assam Association with Assam Provincial Congress, under All India National Congress. Dalbir Sing Lohar was a veteran "Shramik Leader" who held the office of the President of the Assam Tea Workers Union and the President of the Assam Branch of the Indian National Trade Union Congress. He spoke Assamese better than many Assamese leaders and won the appreciations from many Assamese scholars. He took part in the Freedom struggle of India from his student life and suffered imprisonment for several times. Babu Chhabilal Upadhyaya was a true Gandhian leader and he spearheaded Swadeshi movement of Mahatma Gandhi for boycotting foreign goods, denouncing alcohol, opium, *ganja* which ruined Indian families. He acted as a grass-root leader, moved house to house together with Chandranath Sarma and organised Congress Party and collected donation for Tilak Swaraj Fund. He loved Assam, his birthplace, more than Nepal, and for that frank remark that he expressed before the Superintendent of Police he had to court arrest and suffer imprisonment for six months. As a matter of fact, he ignited the idea of nationalism among the Nepalis of the North East and gave them pioneering leadership. He was a great freedom fighter and he led mass people to Quit India movement in 1942 and suffered imprisonment.

The British Government tried its best to prevent Chhabilal Upadhyaya from being a Congress leader. In an encounter with Babu Chhabilal Upadhyaya at Tezpur Polo-field in 1921, the Superintendent of Police (British), Tezpur advised him saying—"Mr. Chhabilal, you are from Nepal which is an independent country, why do you join the Congress and go against the Government of India? Please stop this absurd thing, I would release your seized double barrel gun and the revolver; I will also do anything you want from me". At this Babu Chhabilal Upadhyaya gave a befitting reply by saying—"Well, Nepal might be an independent country, that does not matter to me, at all. What matters to me is Assam, where I am born and where I would die. Assam is my birthplace and India is my country. The freedom movement of India is my movement and therefore, I would not stop doing this movement". Throughout his lif he struggled to bridge up between the Assamese and the Nepalis of Assam. By 1940s, Babu Chhabilal Upadhyaya had become a recognised leader of not only the Nepalis but of whole of Assam. On the 30 September, 1942, a hearty felicitation was accorded to Babu Chhabilal Upadhyaya by the public of Tezpur at Tyagvir Hem Baruah Hall, when Assam's noted poetess, Padmashri Nalini Bala Devi paid homage to him with the following words:

> " Oh, the forebear and hero of the freedom movement of India, being a Nepali you took birth in this beautiful land of Assam, and driven by the sacred dream of serving Assam, your mother land, you joined the crusade of breaking the shackle of foreign rule and sacrificed all you have. Today you are adorned in the heart of every Assamese."[2]

Freedom fighter and *Bagmibir*, Neelamani Phukan poured out his praise on Chhabilal Upadhyaya and Nepali community in the following emotion packed words:

> "Even though an outsider, Shri Chhabilal Upadhyaya became so endeared and respectable figure to the whole country that through his family efforts he turned the Nepali community into an object of pride to the Assamese people. Joining hands with Shri Bishnulal Upadhyaya, former MLA and President of Behali Anchalik Panchayat, many well known persons of his community made our country proud. Today we have keenly realised how this Nepali community has extended its friendship and co-operation to our Assamese community in the trajectory of our common welfare and development."[3]

The above open-hearted praises and warm felicitations extended to the Nepali leaders, *viz.* Chhabilal Upadhyaya and Bishnulal Upadhyaya, by the illustrious sons of Assam make the entire Nepali community living in Assam feel more than happy and grateful to the Asamiya society.

Bhakta Bahadur Pradhan was another Nepali leader who was inspired by Mahatma Gandhi to join his freedom movement. He was one of the top organisers and workers of the Digboi Oil Company. During freedom movement he was twice imprisoned at Dibrugarh and Guwahati and suffered jail for eleven months. In the Second World War he was banished from Assam by British Government under Defence of India Rules for the charge of sedition. He had to leave behind his family, his job and all his properties and leave Assam. He roamed like a beggar but continued to work as freedom fighter in disguise of a monk. After India's independence when he returned home he was given a red carpet welcome and awarded *Tamra-Patra* by Sarat Chandra Sinha, the Chief Minister of Assam as a Freedom Fighter.

Bishnulal Upadhyaya while still a student of Cotton College, Guwahati left his studies and joined freedom movement. One day when organising a Congress demonstration, Police arrested him and produced before the Magistrate. The Magistrate seeing him a young student told him—"You are a student, you have a future; besides that you belong to the Backward Nepali Community. If you agree to sign a bond stating that you would not do such act in future, then I would set you free". To this Bishnulal replied—Whatever I did, I did it knowing fully well and I would continue to do it. Hearing such a curt reply, the Magistrate sentenced him to six months rigorous imprisonment. Kumud Chandra Sarma (Kharel) another vibrant Nepali youngman was also imprisoned for several months and his soap factory was seized for joining the freedom movement. After independence he was also awarded *Tamra Patra*. Bishnulal Upadhyaya was an accomplished writer who wrote both in Nepali and Assamese languages. He wrote many books in Assamese language and inspired Nepali people towards Assamese literature. He wrote—*Mahapurukh Sangkardev Aru Aadi Kavi Bhanu Bhakta* and *Dugaraki Mahan Bibhuti*. He was actively involved in Asom Sahitya Sabha as a life member. He wrote books like, *Khan Mihali,* and *Eri Ahaa Din Bor* and many articles in Assamese language and enriched Assamese literature. Dr. Jogendra Narayan Bhuyan, Maheswar Neog and Satish Chandra Kakati praised Bishnulal Upadhyaya as an accomplished Assamese writer. He was awarded Phulchand Khandelwal award by Asom Sahitya Sabha in recognition of his valuable contribution to Assamese literature. Renowned Assamese litterattuer Homen Borgohain wrote in his letter to Bishnulal Upadhyaya—

> "In Assam the Nepali society is developing fast. They are Assamese despite being Nepalis, and they are Nepalis despite being Assamese. For, they

> are preserving their Nepali culture with pride. Undoubtedly, they will do this in the future too. You are a great representative of Nepali culture and civilization, and at the same time you are a legendary Assamese. You are using your pen in order to bridge up the two cultures. You are one of those great persons whose relentless work has built up this huge Assamese society."[4]

During Quit India Movement of 1942, the Nepalis of various parts of Assam, under the leadership of Babu Chhabilal Upadhyaya, joined hands with Assamese people, took part in processions, held demonstrations and hoisted Indian National Flags at police stations. They suffered police lathi charge, arrest and imprisonment. Among those who suffered imprisonment were—Chhabilal Upadhyaya, Bishnulal Upadhyaya, Hari Prasad Upadhyaya, Dalbir Singh Lohar, Ramlal Upadhyaya, Jainarayan Upadhyaya, Kashinath Luitel, Homnath Guragai, Padma Prasad Dhungel, Balabhadra Chhetri, Narapati Upadhyaya and many others. Demonstrations were held at Rangsali, Behali, Bedeti, Biswanath Charali, Sotea, Jamuguri, Tezpur, Burachhapari, Dhekiajuli etc.

The Question of Khilangia

The All Assam Students Union (AASU) often raise the question of *'Khilanjia'* of Assam, although they have never defined who is a Khilanjia. The Government of Assam have also not clarified who are the Khilanjias. In fact, no one knows exactly what is meant by Khilanjia and yet some people want to enforce them in official use in respect of assigning constitutional rights. The AASU is demanding that hundred per cent seats should be reserved in the state Assembly, Rajya Sabha, Lok Sabha for the Khilanjia

Assamese. In the same way, they are demanding that hundred per cent Government jobs should be allotted to Khilanjias. They say that other persons who are not Khilanjia can exercise franchise but cannot contest any election, they can study but cannot get in any job.

The Clause Six of the Assam Accord made the issue more contentious.

The moot question is—what is the definition of the term Assamese or Khilanjia, or who are, exactly the people that come within the meaning of Khilanjia. There are other terms used together with Khilanjia, these are—"Thalua", indigenous, "local" and "Asamiya". These terms are synonyms and are used interchangeably. The word "Thaluwa" literally means one who resides in Assam permanently. If Khilanjia is synonymous with Thaluwa then Khilanjia means one who is a permanent resident of Assam. In this context, the question of Nepalis and Tea-tribes who are living in Assam permanently comes into consideration—whether they are Khilanjias. These two communities, *viz.*, Nepalis and the Tea-tribes have not only lived for generations in Assam but also identified themselves with Assamese language and culture. They have become same like the Morans, Mataks, Ravas, Tai Ahoms, Koch Raj Bangshis, Karbis etc. who are accepted as Khilanjia Asamiya. If the above named communities who have integrated with Asamiya culture, language and tradition and yet speak their own language and follow their own culture can be considered as Khilanjiyas, then the Nepalis who have also integrated themselves with Assamese language and culture and yet speak Nepali language can also be termed as Khilanjiyas. This apart, if we look at the racial descent we find that both the Nepalis and the above mentioned tribes like Ravas, Cacharis, Morans, Koches, Karbis etc. are all the descendants of the same Kirata race. Noted historians like Suniti Kumar Chatterjee, G.P. Singh, J.N. Choudhuri etc. have said that the Mongolian section of Nepalis of Nepal were descendants of the Kirata race who livd in Kamrupa and North Bengal areas during ancient times. While seeking the answer to the question, let us not forget what Dr. Maheswar Neog, learned historian, meant when he said –"Nepalis are Asamiyas in every way"; let us also recollect what Dr. Tirthanath Sarma hinted at when he said—"a host of the Assamese Gokhains of today including the three time Secretary of the Asom SahityaSobha, Professor Jyotindranath Goswami were the descendants of this Nepali Satradhikar of 16th century of which they were blissfully unaware."[5] Also remember Ambikagiri Rai Choudhury's request to Nepalis to return their mother tongue as Assamese to the census enumerators in 1940; let us also remember Homen Bargohain's statement—"Nepalis have greatly contributed to Assamese literature". Last but not least, let us recall how Mahim Bara, President of Asom Sahitya Sabha hinted at when he said—"Those who remain close to Assamese people during their national festivities as well as their adversities, are the real children of mother Assam; they are the Asamiyas."[6] He spoke this in context with Nepalis of Assam.

Of late, there is a section of Assamese intelligentsia who are in favour of bringing the second or third generation immigrant Muslims (Na-Asamiya[7]) into the greater Assamese Janagosthi who speak Assamese and trying to integrate them with Asamiya. Dr. Nani G. Mahanta writes—

> "Perhaps time is ripe to accommodate the Na-Asamiyas unambiguously into the broader framework of Assamese culture . . . Therefore, the identity discourse of the North East can not keep on cornering the immigrants as an alien for ever and use them as vote bank by the political parties. They are the people whose children are being taught in Assamese medium school and who love to be a part of greater Assamese culture."[8]

The then President of the Asom Sahitya Sabha, Homen Bargohain is a strong upholder of the idea of incorporating the Na-Asamiya (the Assamese name for the immigrants) into the Assamese culture. M.Hussain describes the Na-Asamiya Musalman as the Mymensinghia Muslims from erstwhile East Bengal who are relatively new entrants to the Asamiya nationality along with black-tribals of Assam's tea-plantation. They have been striving hard to assimilate into the larger Asamiya nationality, and have contributed decisively in giving the Asamiya language an absolute and dominant majority status in Assam. The Na-Asamiya Muslims are to be distinguished from the Bengali Muslims of Cachar and they live in the Brahmaputra valley like Asamiya Muslims.[9] Finally, the issue boils down to the fact that the Nepalis in Assam are much older residents than the Na-Asamiya Muslims (Maimensingias) and the tea tribes who came to Assam during middle of nineteenth century, but as far as reliable evidences show that the Nepalis settled down in Assam and assimilated with Asamiya society ever since medieval period.

In this connection, the Government of India, Ministry of Home Affairs, New Delhi constituted a High Level Committee under the chairmanship of former Gauhati High Court Judge Shri B.K.Sharma, to go into the details of the matter and to recommend ways and means for the implementation of the Clause Six of the Assam Accord, vide Notification No. 11012/04/2019-NE VI dated 15 July, 2019. The High Level Committee was also tasked to define the term Assamese, the indigenous people of Assam. Therefore, the High Level Committee issued notices to all NGOs/organisations inviting their suggestions/memorandums. Accordingly, the Nepali/ Gorkha community of Assam represented by Assam Nepali Sahitya Sabha, Nepali Bhasi Kalyan Samiti, Assam Gorkha Sammelan, All Assam Gorkha Students Union, Akhil Assam

Gorkha Sammelan, Bharatiya Gorkha Parisangh (Assam Branch) and other stakeholders, submitted a 400 page joint memorandum dated 20 September, 2019. The memorandum put forward a detailed history of Nepalis migration, settlement and cultural assimilation with Asomiya people together with plausible evidences in support of their claim, and urged upon the High Level Committee to recognise the Nepali/Gorkha community of Assam as an integral part of "Indigenous Assamese society" and provide them constitutional, legislative and administrative safeguards, as given to other Khilanjia communities, to protect, preserve and promote the cultural, social, linguistic identity and heritage of the Nepali/Gorkha community as envisaged under the Clause Six of the Assam Accord.

The High Level Committee, after duly going into the details of the matter, submitted its final report to Shri Sarbananda Sonowal, the Chief Minister of Assam for the needful at his end. The High Level Committee finally recommended that a person who was an inhabitant of Assam on or before 1-1-51 or his descendant will be considered as indigenous (Khilanjiya) of Assam. Thus, the Nepalis who came and settled down in Assam before the 1st January, 1951 and their descendants became eligible for constitutional, legislative and administrative safeguards as the Khilanjias of Assam. The Nepali citizens of India living in Assam for more than two hundred years and their descendants are, therefore eligible to enjoy the benefits as Khilanjias of Assam as envisaged in the **Clause 6** of Assam Accord *viz.*, "Constitutional, legislative and administrative safeguards, as may be appropriate, shall be provided to protect, preserve and promote the cultural, social, linguistic identity and heritage of the **Assamese people**."

NOTES

1. Rupali Phukan Bara (2012). "Jyoti Prasadar Shristirajit Xamannayar Pratitdhani", in *Shailaputri*, Souvenir, Ed. By Uma Pokhrel, p. 241.
2. *Ibid.*, Bishnulal Upadhyaya, p. 40.
3. *Ibid.*, Bishnulal Upadhyaya, pp. 40-41.
4. *Bishnulal Upadhyaya, Byakttwa ra Krititwa*, 2004, Tezpur, p. 11.
5. *Ibid.*, p. 36.
6. *Op cit.*, Viswanath Dipika, Souvenir of 56th Conference.
7. M. Hussain (1993). *The Assam Movement*, Konarak, New Delhi, p. 197.
8. Dr. Nani, G. Mahanta (2007). "Political of Insurgency, Identity and state, Scenario in India". In *Insurgency and Economiv Development in N.E. India*, DVS Publication, Guwahati, p. 29.
9. *Ibid.*, M. Hussain, p. 200.

Index